The AYURVEDIC Vegan KITCHEN

Finding Harmony Through Food

TALYA LUTZKER

Book Publishing Company
Summertown, Tennessee

Book Publishing Company
P.O. Box 99
Summertown, TN 38483
888-260-8458
www.bookpubco.com

Cover and interior design: Scattaregia Design
Photography: Andrew Schmidt
Food styling: Barbara Jefferson, Ron Maxen

ISBN: 978-1-57067-286-6

Printed in the United States

20 19 18 17   4 5 6 7 8 9

Library of Congress Cataloging-in-Publication Data

Lutzker, Talya.
  The Ayurvedic vegan kitchen : finding harmony through food / Talya Lutzker.
      p. cm.
  Includes bibliographical references and index.
  ISBN 978-1-57067-286-6 (pbk.) -- ISBN 978-1-57067-923-0 (e-book)
  1. Vegan cooking. 2. Medicine, Ayurvedic--Popular works. I. Title.
  TX837.L76 2012
  641.5'636--dc23
                            2012021290

Book Publishing Company is a member of Green Press Initiative. We chose to print this title on paper with 100% postconsumer recycled content, processed without chlorine, which saved the following natural resources:

- 49 trees
- 22,361 gallons of water
- 4,959 pounds of greenhouse gases
- 20 million BTU of energy
- 1,417 pounds of solid waste

For more information on Green Press Initiative, visit greenpressinitiative.org.
Environmental impact estimates were made using the Environmental Defense Fund Paper Calculator, edf.org/papercalculator.

Pictured on the cover: Steamed Collard Wraps, p. 108
Pictured on the back cover: Tempeh Reuben, p. 105, with Ayurvedic Home Fries, p. 42;
  Sandy Lane Cherry Pie, p. 163

Contents

Dedication

Just remember one thing:
You are made of light,
And when it is fitting,
You may have to prove it.
– Deepak Chopra

This book is dedicated to my mom.
Thank you for being my biggest fan.

Foreword

I met Talya at the Health and Harmony Festival, where I had a booth to introduce myself as a teacher of Tibetan and ayurvedic medicine and founder of the dhyana Center of Health Sciences. Talya came to my booth for support with her health. I thought, "Here's an inquisitive woman with a lust for life." It was clear that she had a lot of knowledge and a deep willingness to make changes in her life. I consulted with her, read her pulse, suggested some medicinal foods and remedies, and we discussed emotional patterns in relation to health—all according to ayurvedic philosophy.

Eleven years later, I am grateful for all the time we have spent together and for Talya's support through changes in my own health, as well as her vast knowledge of yoga. She loves to share her knowledge and experience with many people; she brought her mom to the dhyana Center (three hours from home) for treatments and always made time to ask questions for others.

In 2002, Talya began studying in my certification programs, including Clinical Foundations of Ayurveda, Aromatherapy, and Ayurvedic Whole Food Nutrition. I knew ayurveda would serve her life path because she has the ability to feel it in her heart, as well as the intellect to see it as a science. Even as a student, she was testing and documenting recipes, finding ways to cook medicinally to support health, and making sure everything tasted like pure love and devotion.

Once Talya was certified as an ayurvedic practitioner, she dove into her clinical internship, consulting with clients. In the years that followed, she refined her skills in pulse assessment, ayurvedic bodywork, and *pancha karma* techniques. She recognized that her passion lay in ayurvedic whole-food nutrition, and she rightly made this her life's focus.

Talya was the first ayurvedic chef at the dhyana Center, and she has been developing her talents ever since. She dedicated her time to cooking beautiful meals for clients in pancha karma retreats, creating menus for each individual's needs, providing ayurvedic catering options, and teaching ayurvedic cooking classes. She's an avid researcher who checks out every detail of a recipe and learns what each individual client needs for his constitution. Talya's great-tasting recipes have earned her quite the reputation. I am sure this is why we sell so many of her books at the dhyana Center.

When Talya is excited about something, she just has to share it. Her book will inspire you to take charge of your health and help you make one small change at a time. The recipes are designed to keep you engaged and to support you in following through with a healthful diet. This cookbook takes you on an exciting journey through ayurveda, and you will use it for years, picking it up for new recipes and as a reference for nutritional practices.

Talya Lutzker is my dear friend, client, student, and colleague. Healthful cooking, eating, and exploring delicious alternatives are natural for her—and she makes it all fun and easy. I have been deeply inspired as I've witnessed her growth, and I am honored to present you with the opening to this brilliant book. *The Ayurvedic Vegan Kitchen* is the perfect balance of knowing your food as medicine and making it taste great.

DeAnna Batdorff

Founder, dhyana Center of Health Sciences
Executive Director, The Aushadi Foundation
www.dhyanacenter.com

Acknowledgments

Let us be together; let us eat together. Let us be vital together;
let us be radiating truth, radiating the light of life.
—The Upanishads

Thank you to everyone who has supported the creation of this book, especially all my dear students, clients, and colleagues. Thank you, Natascha Bruckner, for your talented, generous editing and friendship. Thank you to Beth Colyear for your invaluable support. And thank you, Amey Matthews, for your insightful words on what it means to be vegan. Thank you also to DeAnna Batdorff, Jennifer Hogan, Sarah Medlicott, Heather Nagel, Bernadine Rosso, Todd Stellfox, and Mark Tanaka. You rule.

Most of the recipes in this book were taste-tested by friends, family, and students. Thank you, recipe testers. Your enthusiasm, support, and feedback have been invaluable. My heartfelt thanks to Karen Alreck, Tatiana Bachuretz, Mariposa Bernstein, Erin Bucci, Doña Bumgarner, Shama Cameron, Jill Cavanaugh, Hollie Clausnitzer, Nicole Corren, Mary Davison, Tami Ellis, Katie Engelter, Shelly Errington, Bertha Fierro, Leslie Foster, Deb Fountain, Alison Gee, Miriam Goldberg, Michelle Groenen, Cheryce Gutzmer, Julie Holbrook, Rob Holt, Linda Kimball, Virginia Lefever, Kelly Lehman, Gerald Lutzker, Marti Mariette, CeCe McNeil, Jane and Tim McKay, Laura McShane, Christine Mendonca, Sanjuana Padilla, Molly Rizol, Marcia Rollins, Sita Rucker, Katrina Santos, Miriam Sauer, Andy Schneider, Dave Serna, Shayna Shanes, Sima Shore, Kendell Silveira, Jody Solow, Jet Star, Audra Sternke, Patti Theel, Sara Van Artsdalen, Jil Windsor, Tess Waldo, and Mio Yamashita.

And thank you, Carol Lorente, for holding my hand through the editing process.

CHAPTER 1
What Is Ayurveda?

In the beginning, there was absolute stillness.
— Bri. Maya Tiwari

Ayurveda is one of the oldest documented sciences, originating approximately 5,000 years ago in exotic, colorful India. It's been documented and perfected by ayurvedic experts since its humble beginnings, and is a science so vast it could take lifetimes to absorb all the knowledge and universal understanding it has to offer.

Ayurveda, which, literally translated, means "knowledge of life," is taken from the Sanskrit root words *sat*, which means truth, and *khya*, to know. It is a holistic health-care system that organizes the elements of nature into an understanding of the human body, mind, and spirit—the idea that life is eternally and cosmically unified.

Ayurveda originally came from ancient seers of truth and wisdom called *rishis*, devoted spiritual practitioners who viewed health and wellness as crucial to spiritual life. They founded ayurvedic principles through lifetimes of meditation, physical discipline, and self-observation.

The rishis were masters of consciousness. They witnessed nature's elements within themselves and how the elements tend to move naturally in and out of balance. The rishis' unwavering study was translated into a spiritual, philosophical, and practical code that is now known as ayurveda.

Ayurveda reveres life as a sacred system to which every living thing in the universe belongs. Ayurveda perceives the world through the lens of five elements–ether, air, fire, water, and earth—that are conceived through a dynamic exchange between consciousness, or cosmic energy, and matter, or physicality. The fundamental principle that governs this relationship is called the *gunas*.

Humans experience the gunas through the five senses—sound, touch, sight, taste, and smell—which are extensions of the five elements—ether, air, fire, water, and earth. According to ayurveda, the five elements are the building blocks of life. Ayurveda organizes them into three *doshas* or body types: *vata* (air and ether), *pitta* (fire and water), and *kapha* (water and earth). Doshas are, essentially, the language of ayurvedic medicine.

Symptoms, illnesses and disorders are an excess or depletion of one or more of the doshas; this is how the body communicates that something is out of balance. We are each different; everyone has a constitution unique only to himself. Everyone is made up of all five elements, but the way the predominant characteristics manifest in one person are different from how they manifest in others. One person may be predominantly fire and water (pitta), whereas another may be mostly air and ether (vata). The element that predominates in a person's constitution tends to go out of balance the most and therefore must be tended to most regularly. This is what ayurvedic practitioners mean when they say this is someone's dosha or prakruti.

For example, my prakruti is vata-kapha. The main qualities of vata are cold, dry, light, and subtle—all of which I am—but I am also, at times, congested, heavy, and sad, all signs of kapha. To keep myself in balance, I engage in practices that primarily balance vata. I eat lots of warm foods and spices and try to stay out of the wind. I rub lubricating ayurvedic oils on my skin after I bathe, and I eat lots of plant-based protein so my blood sugar levels stay balanced.

Ayurveda believes that the prakruti or core constitution is a karmic and genetic imprint that cannot be altered. It is living through you, as you, for a divine reason. The physical and mental expression of the doshas through each individual is unique, which means there is no one diet that's right for every single person. In ayurveda, establishing health and well-being means bringing balance to your body and mind. To bring that balance, we need to observe where we are out of balance and introduce foods and lifestyle choices that will bring us back into balance.

The path to health in ayurvedic medicine is to choose foods and recipes that balance your dosha the best. Let's take an example of the gunas using food: *Sattva* is a Sanksrit word describing balance and purity. A food that is light, easy to digest, and has a balancing effect on the mind and body, regardless of one's constitution, is considered *sattvic*. Raw tahini, almonds, sprouts, sweet potato, and mung beans are examples of sattvic foods.

Rajas describes something that is active, enlivening to the senses, and often irritating, acidic, or overstimulating. Coffee, chocolate, spices, and super-salty or sugary foods are *rajasic*. *Tamas* describes a substance that is dull, inert, and heavy. When *tamasic* foods, such as avocado, wheat, onions, and garlic, are eaten in moderation, they provide stability and nourishment. When you eat too much of them, however, you'll feel tired and heavy and want to sleep.

This cookbook will help you determine which dosha predominates in your body, which foods will keep it in balance, and which you should probably avoid, plus recipes that will make it easy to achieve balance and stay there. Each recipe is coded so you can tell at a glance which ones increase, decrease, or balance a dosha. (See "How to Use This Cookbook," page 14, for an explanation of the codes.)

What Is Vegan Ayurveda?

Om Lokah Samasta Sukhino Bhavantu. May all beings everywhere be happy and free.

Vegan ayurveda follows the same nutritional principles of health and balance as traditional ayurveda, but without the use of animal products. This is a significant difference, since cow's milk is worshipped in India, where it is considered the most complete and sattvic food in traditional ayurvedic medicine.

However, for every milk-based food that traditional ayurveda reveres, there is a more than adequate, whole-food vegan alternative that will have a similar effect on your dosha. For example, vegan ayurveda replaces milk, butter, buttermilk, yogurt, and ghee (clarified butter) with equally nourishing foods, such as coconuts, avocados, raw almonds, coconut juice, and raw tahini. Honey, an animal product that is considered a staple of traditional ayurvedic medicine, is substituted with brown rice syrup, dates, frozen fruit juice concentrate, and other natural, plant-based sweeteners.

My intention as an ayurvedic chef is always to prepare delicious food for my clients. And even more so, I want people to feel better *after* they eat. Plant-based foods can reverse such medical issues as high cholesterol and high blood sugar. Lactose-intolerant individuals find a great deal of relief when following a vegan diet. Pitta and kapha types tend to feel less sluggish and less toxic on a vegan diet; they find that their digestion and elimination improves without the heavy, mucous-forming properties of animal products (honey excluded). It can help you keep a natural, healthy body weight and add more energy and vitality to your life.

Ayurveda and the Digestive System

It's not what you eat, it's what you digest that counts.
—Robert E. Svoboda

A healthy digestive system is at the core of ayurvedic medicine because what we eat feeds the blood, and the blood feeds every other body system. Since a vigorous digestive system is key to a healthy, whole body, almost every ayurvedic remedy is geared to making sure the digestive system is operating at its best.

A highly functional digestive system is said to have strong digestive fire, or *agni*, which helps the body absorb what it needs and eliminate the rest. It uses the food we eat to produce vital life fluids, called *ojas*, which feed the body's tissues and maintain vitality, immunity, and radiance.

A fast-paced lifetstyle of overactivity and anxiety, for example, can reduce your digestive ability and deplete your vital fluids. A wholesome diet and adequate rest will feed them, of course, but there are more simple practices you should adopt to help keep your digestive system on track:

- Avoid iced drinks. Drink water that is warm or room temperature.
- Eat moist foods to help reduce gas, bloating, and indigestion. Moisten dry foods with water and healthful oils.
- Eat both raw and cooked food at every meal.
- Avoid table salt, white sugar, white flour, meat, plants sprayed with chemicals, genetically modified foods, alcohol, caffeine, and fried foods. These tend to create toxins in the body.
- Eat most fruit by itself. Don't combine it with other foods.
- Chew your food thoroughly, until it becomes almost liquid in your mouth.
- Don't eat when you're not hungry. Eating when you're not hungry causes gas, indigestion, and weight gain, and can lead to serious digestive disorders.
- Be present with your food. Spend some time each day eating in silence.
- Do not overeat.
- Do not eat late at night.
- Eat what you love. Your food should look good, smell good, and taste good.

This book is a celebration of the benefits of ayurveda and a vegan diet. A vegan lifestyle has been shown to diminish one's carbon footprint and contribute to the health of the planet. Ethical vegans believe that their commitment to veganism causes less suffering to other beings and the world. And, although some people may argue that a vegan diet lacks proper nutrients, it has been shown to be one of the most healthful ways we can nourish our bodies.

Ayurveda can help you feel good by nurturing your nature with dosha-appropriate foods. Why not have those foods be plant-based ones?

CHAPTER 2
The Doshas

Since you are like no other being ever created
since the beginning of time, you are incomparable.
—Brenda Ueland

Ether, air, fire, water, and earth come together to create the three basic constitutional types or doshas: vata, pitta, and kapha. The doshas are active forces that govern all of the biological, psychological, and psychosomatic functions of the body, mind, and spirit, and they possess specific physical, mental, and emotional characteristics. Symptoms or warning signs help us detect imbalances of the doshas before they get out of hand and potentially cause disease.

But when kept in balance through good food choices, environmental surroundings, and lifestyle practices, the doshas work together for the body's benefit. Because the doshas are combinations of elements that can easily become off balance, our awareness and diligence is needed to keep them—and us—sound, sane, and healthy.

Each dosha rules certain aspects of the body. For example, pitta rules the digestive system. It is the force that causes digestive secretions to be produced. If one's digestive fire is weak, ayurveda recommends foods and herbs that increase the pitta dosha, thereby improving the body's digestion, stimulating appetite, and assisting in elimination.

Before we discuss more detailed characteristics of the individual doshas, let's take a quick look at the following chart so you can determine your predominant body type:

A Guide to the Doshas

Qualities	Vata	Pitta	Kapha
The elements:	air and ether	fire and water	water and earth
Your characteristics:	adaptable, light, energetic, talkative, restless	focused, driven, confident, direct, aware	kind, calm, caring, stable, comforting
Your qualities:	dry, cold, light, subtle, changing, clear, mobile	hot, sharp, steamy, oily, focused, sour, fluid, spreading	slow, cool, wet, heavy, stable, moist, oily, dense, juicy, lubricating
Your digestive type:	fast metabolism with poor digestion	easy digestion and elimination	good digestion with slow metabolism
You are:	spiritual, intuitive, creative, talkative, artistic, musical, organized, excited, mutable, enthusiastic	expressive, opinionated, strong, intelligent, powerful, competitive, passionate, precise, adaptable	steady, sensitive, grounded, nurturing, forgiving, stable, reliable, steadfast, generous, patient
Your social type:	communicator, networker, healer, artist	visionary, planner, producer, leader	supporter, provider, mother, father
You prefer to:	travel	create	lounge
To balance, you need:	strength, grounding, warmth, lubrication	calm, cooling, soothing, relaxation	warmth, lightness, movement, motivation

When balanced	Vata	Pitta	Kapha
You are:	communicative, flexible, networking, adaptable, energetic, spiritual, positive, healing, gracious, thoughtful, creative, an initiator	bright, aware, independent, courageous, warm, friendly, ingenious, open-minded, trusting, brilliant, inclusive	peaceful, content, consistent, loyal, compassionate, devoted, nurturing, sweet, calm, reliable

When Out of Balance	Vata	Pitta	Kapha
You are:	nervous, sensitive, uncertain, fearful, impatient, restless, rigid, neurotic, depressed, self-destructive, dishonest, anxious, worried, guilty, indecisive, insecure	reactive, demanding, critical, self-centered, manipulative, vengeful, obsessive, reckless, destructive, arrogant, angry, resentful, jealous, envious, judgmental	possessive, lazy, attached, greedy, stubborn, needy, controlling, unfeeling, reclusive, secretive, comfort-seeking, in despair, depressed, melancholic
You physically experience:	cold, constipation, gas, pain, dry skin, stiff joints	over-heating, heartburn, inflammation, acidity, excessive bleeding	weight gain, phlegm, lethargy, high cholesterol, feeling of heaviness

Nutrition Remedies	Vata	Pitta	Kapha
Tastes that balance:	sweet, salty, sour	sweet, bitter, astringent	bitter, pungent, astringent
Helpful types of foods:	warm, wet, and grounding foods	cool, thirst-quenching foods	warm, light, dry foods
Examples:	cooked root vegetables, soups, stews, oils, minerals, herbal teas, warming spices like ginger	coconut water, fresh juices, green salads, sea vegetables, whole grains, beans, raw seeds, electrolytes, cooling spices like mint	salads, beans, vegetable juices, citrus fruits, fiber, whole grains, motivating spices like rosemary
Dietary recommendations:	Avoid cold foods and skipping meals.	Avoid alcohol, stimulants, overly spicy food.	Avoid salty foods, overeating, overindulging in sweets/desserts.

Vata

Mutable vata comprises air and ether—the concept of empty space—and is always on the move. That is the nature of the air element; change and motion are vata's primary forces.

Vata is often compared to wind. Powerful in its bitter cold, a strong wind can create deep, rough cracks in the earth's surface. It can also be erratic and difficult to nail down. The qualities of light, cold, dry, subtle, and restless are part of vata's innate being. Dryness is exclusive to vata, whereas pitta and kapha share the quality of oiliness. For example, vata body types will tend to have dry skin, while pitta and kapha are prone to oily skin or hair. Whenever there's excessive dryness in the body, it means vata's force is in action.

The love for constant change makes it hard for vata to stick to any sort of routine. Overstimulation and instability are often a result of vata's go-go-go attitude. Vata may eat just to have enough energy for the next activity on their already too long to-do list.

Although vata may have been painfully shy as a child, vata still loves excitement and is often the center of attention because of their chatty nature. Vata's energy comes in spurts, and they tire easily, making them start many projects while finishing few.

Vata tends to go to extremes. They can be overly rigid, uptight, and busy. Vata types will try to sustain crazy amounts of energy through the use of caffeine, chocolate, and stimulants, only to find that exhaustion is inevitable and that a feeling of profound depression often follows.

Vata sleeps lightly, strongly prefers variety over routine, has a hard time sitting still, and loves the sun. Although vata types have all the answers, they sometimes appear to be airheads—such as when they are so "cosmically connected" that they can't remember what they were just talking about.

With a thin, narrow frame, light bone structure, and cold extremities, vata's nervous system is especially sensitive, as the body is not very well insulated. It is common for vata to experience bouts of cracking joints, insomnia, weak digestion, irregular elimination, and poor endurance, and to show a special sensitivity to pain and loud noises. Vata is excreted from the body through the same sort of energy this element exhibits—gas and nervous energy. Vata's short-term memory is fine, but memory loss is a common sign of vata imbalance. Vata rules the spatial cavities of the body—indicative of its air and ether—which include the colon, heart, lungs, bladder, bones, bone marrow, brain, and nervous system.

Autumn, the driest season, is the time of year when vata increases and is most apt to be challenging, so it's a perfect time for vata to partake in warm, hydrating, oily foods.

While all of this motion is vital for health, without stability vata is out of control. Emotionally, vata exists in the heady realm of fear, anxiety, worry, guilt, and indecision. Nervous, introspective, spiritual, and uncertain, vata may take things too seriously, thereby creating unnecessary drama and episodes of sensitive fragility. Vata needs to know its own worth and march to the beat of its own drum. Because they are easily influenced and have difficulty focusing on their own rhythm, vata types may indulge in myriad addictive behaviors. Learning how to let go, be decisive, and own their self-worth is what vata needs to thrive.

For specific foods that are best for balancing vata, see page 19.

Pitta

Powerful pitta is born from the relationship between fire and water, so its characteristics are just what one would expect from such a union: pitta is the only dosha that exudes heat and all that that implies. Pitta's job is to transform and assimilate, and to balance the opposing forces of vata's cold, constant movement with kapha's cool, stable passivity.

Any amount of heat, acidity, or inflammation is related to pitta, as is demonstrated by symptoms like heartburn and excessive perspiration. But "heat" doesn't apply just to temperature. Pitta thrives on challenge, which calls forth its naturally ambitious and competitive nature. Focused, determined, and driven, pitta types are visionary leaders who love to be the boss. They are demanding, precise, opinionated, highly intelligent, and brilliantly sharp. They apply the same intensity to play as they do to work. Pitta rules the middle, most active, and productive time of life, from puberty to menopause.

When pitta types are in touch with their life purpose and passions—and they usually are—they have a powerful creative spark that must be given a voice. They are blessed with stamina, strong will, initiative, and a deeply creative spirit. Good at solving problems and planning, pitta has a quick, clear memory. Watch out when you cross pitta though, as its strong, stubborn, inner warrior may give rise to anger, irritability, control, or defensiveness. It is common for pitta to exude jealousy, judgment, and even hatred, but when in balance, pitta reflects qualities of joy, freedom, reverence, trust, and love.

One way pitta is eliminated is through bile, a soapy green liquid created in the liver and stored in the gall bladder. Areas of the body where water and fire congregate include all regions of the digestive system, especially the liver and spleen. Pitta also rules the endocrine system, hormones, blood, eyes, skin, sweat glands, and brain.

Pitta types tend to be medium built, muscular people with bright eyes, oily skin, and athletic tendencies. They are sensitive to heat, so they are often thirsty, and are encouraged to quench their thirst with cool, hydrating drinks. Strong digestion and elimination come easy to them. They will often experience vivid, colorful dreams with potentially disturbing themes that may lead them to adopt a variety of numbing, addictive habits. Prone to workaholism, pitta needs to keep a watch on its kidney health to avoid adrenal burnout. Proper amounts of rest, relaxation, and hydration will do the trick, if pitta can find the time to chill out for a while.

As you can probably guess, summer is pitta's season. Have you ever noticed that you get a "second wind" around 10 p.m.? That's the solar energy of pitta coming to life.

For specific foods that are best for balancing pitta, see page 22.

Kapha

Kapha is the dosha of earth and water. Its qualities are likened to those of mud, since that is what you get when you mix earth and water. However, kapha is also the element that helps keep liquids (water) and solids (earth) in proper proportion and perspective. Kapha is the only dosha that possesses the quality of heaviness; both vata and pitta are light in nature. Cool, dense, stable, oily, slow, and soft, kapha provides lubrication and a capacity to store vital energy. Kapha must not become too wet or too static, or too much mucus, stagnancy, and inertia may accumulate.

Kapha types are the ones you want to call when times are tough. Natural nurturers and protectors, kaphas are laid-back, grounded individuals who excel at listening, loving, forgiving, mothering, providing, and staying even-keeled in the face of stress. They are stable, thorough, firm in their beliefs, stubborn, and resistant to change. They love their food and security and are hesitant to give up either one. When they apply themselves, they tend to be natural athletes.

Usually heavyset with good musculature, kapha is the envy of all vata and pitta for its soft, wavy, lustrous hair, beautiful smooth skin, and large eyes. Kapha types are strong, thick, cool, and moist, tending to prefer warm, dry environments. Their appetite is steady, their metabolism slow, and elimination regular. They are blessed with endurance, memory, and the ability to sleep long hours. They are famous for being able to make lots of money and keep it. Exercise is perhaps the best thing for kapha, but it often lacks the motivation to do it. It's important for kapha types not to overeat because they are prone to gaining weight, which is a shame because they love food so much.

Kapha is expelled from the body in the form of mucus, which it may have in excess when out of balance. Congestion, edema, fatigue, flatulence, and fluid retention prevail when kapha is too wet, sticky, slimy, cool, or dense. The kapha time of life is from infancy to puberty, the time of greatest growth. Babies are exemplary of healthy kapha, all fat and juicy and full of growth hormones.

It deeply behooves kapha types to engage their creative and adventurous sides, as newness and change of routine is what motivates and enlivens their spirits. The greatest danger for kapha is getting stuck in a rut, when it's easy to settle into attachment, dullness, and depression. The classic couch potato, kapha can easily become lost in isolation, sadness, melancholy, grief, and greed. Vigorous exercise, creative projects, and variety will help kapha rediscover its sattvic nature of loyalty, generosity, devotion, wisdom, and abundance. Although they thrive on being needed by others, loving and giving to themselves is kapha's deepest source of nourishment.

For specific foods that are best for balancing kapha, see page 25.

CHAPTER 3
The Six Tastes of Ayurveda

I've grown new vegetables just to see what they taste like.
—Barbara Kingsolver

Taste, called *rasa* in Sanskrit, is the key to understanding ayurvedic nutrition. It is why certain foods influence some people's digestion in a positive way while not for others.

In terms of importance, taste is second only to water—the element without which taste would not exist. (If the tongue is dry, it cannot taste.) Rasa is the immediate taste on the tongue, the one we remember, and the immediate experience of how that particular taste influences the body. Taste is made from the same five elements that comprise the doshas—ether, air, fire, water, and earth—and a rasa may be sweet, sour, salty, pungent, bitter, or astringent. Its corresponding short-term effect will have a direct influence on vata, pitta, and kapha.

Rasa also translates as "emotion," since what is taste to the tongue is emotion to the mind. For example, we often feel really happy when we are given something sweet. Yet we may feel somewhat bitter about having to finish all the greens on our plate. We may go to food specifically for the feeling it lends to our state of being, not caring quite as much about the flavor it emits on the tongue. Like too much of any good thing, even a taste that balances your dosha should be taken in moderation.

Each taste has a direct energetic effect on digestion, creating either a heating or a cooling sensation. This action on the digestive system, called *virya*, may be felt immediately after tasting a food, or some time later. For example, a sweet mango has a heating virya and tends to enhance digestive function. A medjool date is also sweet, but it has a cooling virya and tends to slow digestive function. You may feel more full five minutes after eating the date than five minutes after eating the same amount of mango, because the date is denser and has a heavier, more cooling effect on the digestive system.

Every taste has a long-term effect on our metabolism after digestion is complete, and all the nutrients have been assimilated in the tissues. This effect is known as *vipak* and is either sweet, sour, or pungent. The vipak of sweet is deeply nutritive and building; the vipak of sour enhances digestive fire, and the vipak of pungent creates increased elimination.

These qualities will be best understood through personal experience and practice. You will discover more about your true nature by noticing how foods make you feel as you digest them. Noticing how you feel is quite possibly your most powerful tool for healing in ayurveda.

It should be noted here that there are some rare and unexplainable mysteries and exceptions to these ayurvedic rules. One is that certain foods create an action on the body that is contradictory to its taste. For example, lemon is sour and should therefore have a warming virya, but it is cooling to the body. Turmeric, which is bitter and should therefore have a cooling virya, is heating.

How to Use This Cookbook

The key to ayurvedic cooking is to look for recipes that decrease, pacify, or balance your dosha. In this cookbook, the particular effect of a recipe on the doshas is noted at the top of every recipe page and included with all of the recipe variations.

The Six Rasas

Sweet (*Madhura*) decreases vata and pitta, increases kapha

Sweet has a cooling virya, with some exceptions, and a sweet vipak. Of all the six tastes, sweet is the most grounding and nourishing. It's balancing to vata and pitta and, when eaten in moderation, promotes longevity, strength, and healthy bodily fluids and tissues. It's the taste to emphasize for someone who is trying to gain weight, as it will quickly increase kapha when taken in excess. Its heavy, oily, moist qualities tend to slow down digestion, so it's often suggested in ayurveda to eat dessert first. The sweet taste abounds in foods such as wheat, rice, maple syrup, brown rice syrup, agave nectar, dates, licorice root, and slippery elm bark.

Salty (*Lavana*) decreases vata, increases pitta and kapha

The salty taste has a heating virya and a sweet vipak. Salt is grounding and moistening, which makes it best for vata. Its warmth and unctuousness helps vata stay grounded and hydrated, but its heat may aggravate pitta. Kapha will be attracted to the warmth of salty flavors, but this flavor tends to promote more weight gain and water retention than kapha really wants. Salt stimulates digestion, helps maintain proper electrolyte balance, softens tissues, and has a mildly laxative effect when taken in moderation. Sea vegetables, salt, tamari, black olives, and processed foods are laden with the salty rasa.

Sour (*Amla*) decreases vata, increases pitta and kapha

Sour's heating virya is followed by a warming, sour vipak. The sour taste stimulates appetite and saliva production, and is stabilizing in its light, heating, and oily properties. But it should be eaten in moderation, for its refreshing influence is strong, and a little bit goes a long way. Sour balances vata, but the sour taste tends to unbalance pitta with heat, and can suffocate kapha with its slippery, grounding nature. Sour improves appetite, digestion, and elimination, and includes such foods as lemons, ume plum, amla berry (sour Indian gooseberry), vinegars, and pickled and fermented foods.

Pungent (*Katu*) increases vata and pitta, decreases kapha

Air and fire give rise to the pungent rasa whose virya is heating and vipak is pungent. The hottest of all the rasas, the pungent taste improves appetite, clears sinuses, stimulates blood circulation, and motivates the senses. The pungent rasa will taste hot and stay hot from start to finish, thereby benefiting kapha more than vata. The pungent taste, with its light and dry qualities, will aggravate pitta quickly. It is sure to balance wet, heavy kapha, but it can be too hot and dry for vata when taken in excess or paired with too many other drying foods. Vata does best when the pungent taste is combined with sour, sweet, or salty foods. Fresh ginger, hot peppers, onions, garlic, mustard, and hot spices all share the quality of pungency.

Bitter (*Tikta*) increases vata, decreases pitta and kapha

Of the six tastes, bitter is the coolest and lightest, making it best for pitta and least effective for vata, especially when taken without a proper balance of other tastes. Air and ether comprise this rasa, whose virya is cooling and whose vipak is pungent, making it quite cooling in the short term, but warming in the big picture. Kapha benefits from foods like dark leafy greens that abound with the bitter taste while providing calming magnesium and calcium. Dandelion root, turmeric, and fenugreek are also great sources of bitterness with cool and drying qualities.

Be careful to avoid the bitter taste in excess, as it's known to create immediate coldness that can bring on bouts of grief and depression. Like sour, a little goes a long way. Make the bitter rasa a regular part of your meals but in small amounts. It will enhance the flavor of other foods and help to gently purify and cleanse the body.

Astringent (*Kasaya*) increases vata, decreases pitta and kapha

Cool, dry, and light, the astringent rasa has a cooling virya and a pungent vipak. It is less cold than bitter but very dry and firm, which makes it a taste for vata to avoid. Many beans and legumes are astringent in nature, as are broccoli and cauliflower, all of which are known to create gas and thus aggravate the vata dosha.

Pitta will benefit from the astringent taste's coolness, while its dry, light qualities help balance kapha. The constrictive nature of the astringent taste will also slow down digestion. Green grapes, unripe bananas, cranberries, pomegranates, alfalfa sprouts, green beans, and okra all exhibit the astringent taste. You will know this taste when it makes your mouth pucker and feel dried out.

CHAPTER 4
Foods for Your Dosha

The food is Brahma (creative energy). Its essence is Vishnu (sustainable energy).
The eater is Shiva (destructive and restorative energy). No sickness due to food
can come to one who eats with this knowledge.
—Sanskrit blessing

Once you've determined your dosha, your next step to health and vitality is to incorporate the right foods into your diet.

How to Balance Vata with Nutrition

Vata should follow a warm, wet, oily, hydrating, grounding diet. Warm, cooked whole grains, soups, stews, spices, hot teas, curries, fresh oils, raw nuts, and lecithin powder should make up the bulk of vata's diet. Go light on yeast breads and most raw foods because of the high amount of digestive fire they require; a diet that's 25 percent raw and 75 percent cooked food is usually about right. In warmer, more humid climates and in summer, however, vata types can indulge in more raw food. It's better for vata to lean on warm, cooked foods in winter and in colder climates.

Beans should be avoided because of their astringent nature, unless they are part of an oily, well-spiced dish, such as Kitchari (page 116), so cook them with lots of cumin, ginger, spices, and sea vegetables. Soak beans before cooking to make them easier to digest.

Since vata's digestive fire tends to be weak, it's best to avoid poor food combinations. For example, eat fresh fruit by itself, not with other foods, and stick with sweet juicy fruits, rehydrated dried fruits, stewed fruits, and fruit sauces.

Salty is the most beneficial taste for vata because of its warming, earthy, unctuous qualities. Sour foods like ume plum and Raw Sauerkraut (page 82) also benefit vata when eaten in moderation. Most herbs and spices are good for vata because of their warming qualities. Too many pungent spices can be drying and stimulating, so use fresh herbs whenever possible.

Most nuts and seeds are good for vata because of their sweet, heavy, oily nature, but raw, soaked, and sprouted nuts are best. Avoid eating too many raw nuts and seeds because they will be hard to digest in large amounts.

Infuse your meals with superfoods, such as spirulina, chia seeds, goji berries, and aloe vera juice, especially in the afternoons, when vata is increased.

Sweet balances vata, but too much of a good thing is too much. Enjoy sweetness through whole grains, root vegetables, and warm meals, in addition to sweet treats.

More nutrition tips for vata:
- Vata meals should be so wet or oily that they must be served in bowls. Put raw oil over your foods every day; 1 to 2 tablespoons of oil over a bowl of soup or oatmeal feels nourishing and helps keep your skin, joints, and tissues lubricated.
- Sip hot tea or broth with meals.
- Enhance your food with lecithin powder, ground nuts or seeds, and spices.
- Add warm nut and seed milks to cereal.

Vata should avoid: black-eyed peas, broccoli, Brussels sprouts, cabbage, cauliflower, corn, cranberries, dried fruits, millet, pinto beans, pomegranates, raw onions, split peas, watermelon, and white sugar.

Also avoid all astringent, dry, cold, iced, and icy foods. Stay away from excess amounts of citrus fruits, cold cereal, crackers, dry toast, gluten, pickled foods, popcorn, most vinegars, and stimulants, such as coffee, alcohol, and white sugar.

Foods for Vata

Vegetables

artichokes	garlic	mung bean sprouts	spinach, cooked
asparagus	green beans	mustard greens	squash
beets	Jerusalem artichokes	okra	turnips
bok choy	jicama	onions, cooked	sweet potatoes
carrots	kale	parsnips	watercress
celery	leeks	pumpkin	zucchini
fennel root		radishes	

Fruits

acai, sweet	coconut	lime	pineapple
apricots	dates	mangoes	plums
avocados	figs	nectarines	raisins
bananas	goji berries	papaya	rhubarb, sweet
blueberries	grapes, sweet	peaches	tamarind
cherries	kiwifruit	persimmon, sweet	tangerines

Grains

amaranth	brown rice breads	rice, all varieties
brown rice	oats	sprouted wheat

Beans and Legumes

adzuki	mung beans,	spicy tofu
black beans	split or whole	tempeh
fresh fava beans	red lentils	

Nuts and Seeds

almonds, with skins removed	chia seeds	pistachios	pumpkin seeds
brazil nuts	flaxseeds, soaked	poppy seeds	sesame seeds
cashews	macadamia nuts	psyllium seeds, in moderation	sprouted peanuts
	pine nuts		sunflower seeds

Spices and Herbs

asafetida	clove	lemongrass	rose
basil	coriander, ground	mace	saffron
bay leaf	cumin, ground	marjoram	tamarind
caraway seeds	cumin seeds	mint, fresh	thyme
cardamom	fennel seeds	nutmeg	turmeric
cilantro, fresh	garlic, fresh	rosemary, fresh	vanilla bean
cinnamon	ginger, fresh and ground		

Oils and Condiments

black olives	olive oil, cold-pressed and extra-virgin	sea vegetables	sunflower oil
Bragg Liquid Aminos or coconut aminos	purple olives	sesame oil	Thai green curry paste
maca root powder	salt	spirulina, best in summer	ume plum vinegar
miso			

Sweeteners

raw agave nectar	dates	dried figs, reconstituted	maple syrup
brown rice syrup	date sugar		molasses
coconut nectar	dehydrated cane juice	jaggery	raisins, soaked
coconut sugar			

How to Balance Pitta with Nutrition

Although known for an "iron stomach" that can digest just about anything, pitta will fare best with a cool, hydrating diet abundant in fresh fruits, vegetable juices, beans, and cooling grains such as basmati rice, wheat berries, and oats. Cooling spices like mint, fennel, dill, parsley, saffron, coriander, and turmeric soothe and neutralize acidic pitta. Pitta thrives on smooth coconut oil, wheatgrass, mineralizing sea vegetables, and raw, protein-rich seeds like hemp, chia, and sunflower. Unleavened breads are best.

Soaked, raw grains are cooling, grounding, and will give you enduring energy. Likewise, soak beans before cooking whenever possible—or sprout them and steam them so they're easier to digest. Cooked beans are pitta's friend, especially when topped with fresh sprouts and avocado.

Pitta should be careful not to rely too heavily on oily nuts, salty snacks, or stimulants since pitta is already fairly stimulated by life. Green tea, maple syrup, brown rice syrup, and Rice Milk (page 34) are good staples to keep around. Pitta does well on a half-raw, half-cooked diet and may lean more heavily on the raw side, especially in summer and in warm climates.

Sweet balances pitta but, like vata, an intense amount of sweet will cause an imbalance. That being said, raw chocolate is worlds better for you than anything processed. Raw, unprocessed desserts are your best choice.

More nutrition tips for pitta:
- Eat small, frequent meals. Keep snacks with you at all times.
- Stick to sweet juicy fruits. Avoid all sour fruits except lime for its cooling nature.
- Sip cool water throughout the day.
- Add small amounts of raw oils to your food, and eat fats accompanied by high-fiber foods, such as vegetables, grains, and seeds.
- Enhance your meals with sprouts and superfoods such as sea vegetables, spirulina, wheatgrass, and blue-green algae. These foods will replenish your spirit and are also high in protein.
- Chew your food completely.
- Give thanks before and after you eat.

Pitta should avoid: dried ginger, eggplant, raw garlic, grapefruit, horseradish, millet, olives, onions, papaya, pecans, poppy seeds, quinoa, radishes, rye, sesame oil, sour fruits, spicy foods, turnips, oily foods, fried foods, and pungent herbs or spices.

Avoid excessive amounts of sour fermented foods, salty foods, processed foods, roasted nuts and seeds, chiles, peppers, peanuts, and peanut butter.

Foods for Pitta

Vegetables

alfalfa sprouts	cauliflower	dandelion greens	red potatoes
asparagus	carrot,	green beans	rutabaga
artichokes	in moderation	Jerusalem artichokes	squash
beets, in moderation	celery	jicama	spinach, raw,
broccoli	collard greens	kale	in moderation
Brussels sprouts	corn, fresh	lettuce	sunflower sprouts
cabbage	cucumbers	mushrooms	sweet potatoes
			zucchini

Fruits

acai, sweet	coconut	mangoes	pineapple, sweet
avocados	dates	melons	plums
bananas,	figs	oranges, sweet	pomegranates
in moderation	grapes, sweet	peaches	tangerines
blueberries	guava, sweet	pears	watermelon
cherries, sweet	limes	persimmons, sweet	

Grains

barley	buckwheat groats,	oat groats, soaked	white rice
basmati rice	soaked	oats	sprouted wheat

Beans and Legumes

adzuki	chickpeas	lima beans	pinto beans
black beans	fresh fava beans	mung beans,	split peas
black lentils	kidney beans	split or whole	tofu

Nuts and Seeds

almonds, soaked	hempseeds,
chia seeds	in moderation
flaxseeds	sunflower seeds

Spices and Herbs

basil, fresh	coriander, ground	lavender flowers	rose
caraway seeds,	cumin, ground	lemongrass	saffron
in moderation	cumin seeds	mint, fresh and dried	tulsi
cardamom	dill, fresh and dried	parsley,	turmeric
cilantro, fresh	fennel seeds	fresh and dried	vanilla bean
cinnamon	ginger, fresh		

Oils and Condiments

avocado oil	coconut vinegar	maca root powder	wheatgrass
blue-green algae	flaxseed oil	sea vegetables	Vitamineral Green
coconut oil	hempseed oil	spirulina	

Sweeteners

barley malt syrup	dates	frozen fruit juice
brown rice syrup	date sugar	concentrate
coconut nectar	fresh fruit	maple syrup
coconut sugar		

How to Balance Kapha with Nutrition

Kapha thrives on a light, low-fat, high-fiber diet and should emphasize pungent, bitter, and astringent tastes found in hot, light, spicy foods. Light vegetables, such as cabbage, asparagus and artichokes, will serve kapha well, alongside warming whole grains, such as quinoa, millet, amaranth, oat bran, barley, and rye. Pair grains with lots of fresh vegetables, spicy sprouts, and spices. Most herbs and spices are good for kapha because of their warming, pungent qualities; fresh basil, parsley, cilantro, garlic, arugula, and ginger should be a large part of kapha's seasoning repertoire. Soak beans before cooking to make them easier to digest, and cook them with cumin, ginger, spices, and sea vegetables to help reduce gas and bloating.

About 40 percent raw foods, 60 percent cooked foods is a good diet ratio for kapha, although they can eat more raw foods in the summer and more cooked in the winter.

Salads, sprouts, warm teas, sprouted corn tortillas, flourless breads, raw seeds, fresh vegetable juices, beans, sunflower oil, and flaxseed oil help balance blood sugar levels and maintain stable energy.

Enhance kapha's meals with condiments, such as ground flaxseeds, ginger, onions, and spicy sprouts. One or two tablespoons can be sprinkled over grains, steamed vegetables, soups, and salads.

Kapha is increased by the sweet taste, so most sweeteners should be avoided. Low-glycemic sweeteners, such as Jerusalem artichoke syrup, raw yacon syrup, and frozen fruit juice concentrate are the favored sweeteners for kapha.

More nutrition tips for kapha:
- Because kapha can find it easy to gain weight, correct portion size is important for them to remember. (See "Know Your Serving Size," page 29.)
- Sip hot ginger tea or unsalted broth with meals.
- Eat high-fiber, blood sugar-balancing foods, such as nopal cactus, spirulina, ground flaxseeds, whole grains, and lentils.
- Eat dry, light fruits with astringent qualities, such as grapes, berries, and pomegranate seeds.
- Eat only when hungry.
- Do not eat late at night.

Chai, page 32, with star anise

Vegan Mango Lassi, page 40

Kapha should avoid: avocado, banana, brown rice syrup, processed carbohydrates, including sticky-sweet desserts, dates, figs, excessively sweet and sour fruits, iced drinks, most melons, molasses, oats, most nuts, olives, tomatoes, wheat, white sugar, yeast, and zucchini.

Foods for Kapha

Vegetables

artichokes	cabbage	horseradish	onions, raw
arugula	carrots	Jerusalem artichokes	peas
asparagus	cauliflower	kale	radishes
bell peppers	corn, fresh	kohlrabi	spinach
bok choy	collard greens	lettuce	squash
broccoli	dandelion greens	leeks, raw	sprouts
Brussels sprouts	garlic	mustard greens	turnips
burdock root	green beans		

Fruits

acai, unsweetened	coconut, dried	grapes	persimmons, hard
apricots	cranberries	lemons	pomegranates
berries	dried fruits,	mangoes	tangerines
cherries	in moderation	pears	

Grains

Basmati Rice	corn	quinoa	sprouted grain
buckwheat	millet	rye	breads, toasted

Beans and Legumes

adzuki	mung beans,	red lentils	spicy tofu
black beans	split or whole	split green and	tempeh,
chickpeas	pinto beans	yellow lentils	in moderation
fresh fava beans			

Nuts and Seeds

almonds, soaked	flaxseeds	poppy seeds	pumpkin seeds
chia seeds,	hempseeds,	psyllium seeds	sunflower seeds
in moderation	in moderation		

Spices and Herbs

allspice	clove	lavender flower	rose
anise	coriander, ground	mace	saffron
asafetida	cumin, ground	marjoram	sage
basil	cumin seeds	mint, fresh	tamarind
bay leaf	fennel seeds,	and dried	tarragon
black pepper	in moderation	neem	thyme
caraway seeds	garlic, fresh	nutmeg	tulsi
cardamom	ginger, fresh and	orange peel	turmeric
cayenne	ground	raspberry leaf	vanilla bean
cinnamon	hibiscus	rosemary, fresh	

Oils and Condiments

blue-green algae	coconut oil,	nopal cactus	spicy sprouts
chia seeds, sprouted	in moderation	sunflower oil	spirulina
cider vinegar	flaxseed oil	sea vegetables	Vitamineral Green
coconut aminos,	flaxseeds, ground		
in moderation	and whole		

Sweeteners

coconut nectar,	fresh fruits	Jerusalem	raw yacon syrup
in small amounts	frozen fruit juice	artichoke syrup	stevia
dried fruits	concentrate, like		
	apple or grape		

CHAPTER 5
Before You Begin

Thank you for this food, this food, this glorious, glorious food,
And the animals, and the vegetables, and the minerals that made it possible.
—Patricia McKernon

Almost all of the ingredients for the recipes in this book can be found at farmers' markets, natural food stores, the organic section of grocery stores and supermarkets, and online. Following are some shopping tips for purchasing the whole foods you'll need to cook ayurvedic recipes:

Pick your produce wisely. Choose organic or unsprayed, local, seasonal produce whenever possible.

Read food labels. Even seemingly innocent items such as raw granola and tempeh may not be vegan or gluten-free (which can be important for vata and kapha). Make sure to buy the least adulterated version of every ingredient to avoid additives and retain the power to season your meals as you please.

Say no to GMOs. Genetically modified organisms, or GMOs, are a result of genetic engineering, which transfers the genes of one plant or species to another. The long-term health impact of genetically modified foods is yet to be determined. If a processed or packaged food doesn't claim to be GMO-free, assume that it isn't. Common GMO plants are canola, potato, corn, wheat, tomatoes, and soy.

Buy in bulk. Most natural food stores and many supermarkets have bulk foods sections where you can obtain whole grains, legumes, raw nuts, and raw seeds. It is cheaper to buy in bulk, and it cuts down on packaging, particularly if you bring bags from home.

Buy fair trade. Fair trade is a way of doing business in the spirit of social justice. Western markets join forces with food growers in developing countries, who benefit by earning better pay and enjoying improved trade conditions. Some examples of products that are commonly fair-traded are chocolate, coffee, yerba maté, cacao powder, fresh fruits, and flowers.

Keep it clean. Good-quality purified water—free of chemicals, contaminants, and harmful bacteria—is key to health, vitality, and really great food. Use only purified water in the recipes in this cookbook.

Use the right salt. Avoid kosher or table salt, which is sodium chloride that is cheap, bleached, processed, and devoid of many of the minerals in fresh sea salt or high-quality crystal salt. Use Celtic salt, Himalayan pink salt, Lima sea salt, fleur de sel, or Hawaiian sea salt.

Before you start cooking:

- Read "How to Use This Cookbook" (see page 14) so you will be able to tell which recipes are best for balancing your dosha.
- Leave the peels on vegetables such as beets, carrots, cucumbers, ginger, parsnips, radishes, red potatoes, and sweet potatoes, unless specified otherwise.
- Likewise, leave the peels on fruits such as apples and pears unless specified otherwise. Use the unsweetened varieties of dried fruits.
- Use the whole plant, including the stems, for vegetables such as bok choy, cilantro, collard greens, dandelion greens, green onions, leeks, kale, and spinach.
- Use only raw nuts and seeds, including raw nut and seed butters, unless the recipe specifies otherwise.
- Unless otherwise specified, use only raw, unrefined, organic, cold- or expeller-pressed oils, such as extra-virgin coconut oil and olive oil, grapeseed oil, and sunflower oil. Likewise, use only raw cider vinegar and raw agave nectar.
- A high-powered, high-speed blender is recommended for use in recipes that call for a blender, but a regular home blender will work. (You may have to process some recipes in batches if they don't fit in the blender jar.)
- See the Glossary (page 164) if you need definitions of some of the other ingredients called for in this cookbook.

Know Your Serving Size

A serving size will vary based on your body size. In ayurveda, a serving size is referred to as an *anjali*. A simple way to determine the right amount of food for you at any one meal is to put your hands together so that they form a "bowl" (palms up, outer edges of your hands touching). The amount of food you can hold in this bowl is, according to ayurveda, the correct amount of food at one meal to satisfy your body. It's also the amount of food that will make you feel good after eating and help you maintain your natural body weight.

CHAPTER 6

Drinks, Teas, and Tonics

DRINKS, TEAS, AND TONICS ARE SIMPLE SOURCES OF NUTRITION and easy ways to explore food as medicine. When a beverage is balancing for you, it will feel appropriately nourishing, cleansing, cooling, or warming. You are likely to enjoy it immensely and reap the benefits its "medicine" has to offer.

Blending makes large quantities of alkaline-forming fruits and vegetables bio-available and easily digestible. Fresh fruits and juices balance all of the doshas, so it's helpful to know which ones are best for your constitutional type. Most store-bought fruit juices should be diluted with water because of their intense sweetness, acidity, and lack of fiber.

Juices and Teas that Balance Vata
Aloe vera, carrot, Chai (page 32), chamomile, coconut, fresh ginger, lavender, licorice root, lime, mango, fresh mint, papaya, pineapple, rooibos, rose, slippery elm bark, and tulsi

Juices and Teas that Balance Pitta
Aloe vera, apple, chamomile, chrysanthemum, coconut, dandelion root, grape, green vegetable, lavender, lime, mint, mango, pear, pomegranate, raspberry leaf, tulsi, and watermelon

Juices and Teas that Balance Kapha
Aloe vera, chamomile, cranberry, ginger, hibiscus, lavender, lemon, nettle, mint, pear, pomegranate, raspberry leaf, tulsi, and vegetable juices

Chai

balances vata, pitta, and kapha

Preparation Time: 20 minutes
Yield: About 30 (1-cup) servings

SEE PHOTO FACING PAGE 24.

The health-promoting spice blend in this traditional ayurvedic tea is a natural digestive-aid extravaganza. Chai is delicious, stimulating, and energizing, and it also warms your heart and soul.

Spice mix

¼ cup cardamom pod or cardamom seeds

¼ cup dried licorice root or anise seeds

¼ cup cinnamon chips (see Note), or 4 (3-inch) cinnamon sticks

¼ cup coriander seeds

2 tablespoons whole cloves

2 tablespoons black peppercorns

1 tablespoon fennel seeds

Chai

1 cup water

1 (1-inch) piece fresh ginger, cut into thin slices

1 teaspoon Spice Mix (above)

1 to 2 tablespoons Almond Milk (page 34), Oat Milk (page 38), Rice Milk (page 34), or prepared vegan milk of your choice

1 teaspoon maple syrup or brown rice syrup

⅛ teaspoon ground nutmeg (optional)

To make the spice mix, combine all the ingredients in a jar.

To make the chai, bring the water and ginger to a boil in a medium saucepan. Add 1 teaspoon of the spice mix. Decrease the heat. Simmer for 10 to 15 minutes. Strain the tea into a cup. Stir in the Almond Milk, maple syrup, and optional nutmeg.

Note: Cinnamon chips are available in the bulk spice section of some natural food stores, or they can be purchased online. (See Resources, page 169.)

Mocha Chai
(balances vata and kapha, increases pitta slightly): Before adding the Almond Milk, stir in 1 teaspoon of cacao powder or carob powder. Add 2 teaspoons of the maple syrup.

Caffeinated Chai
(increases vata and pitta, decreases kapha): Before adding the Almond Milk, add 1 tea bag of organic black tea, green tea, or yerba maté. Let the tea steep for 5 to 7 minutes. Remove and discard the tea bag.

Ginger Café Latte

balances vata, pitta, and kapha

Preparation Time: 10 minutes
Yield: 1 (1-cup) serving

This is one of my favorite hot drinks and, while not a complete substitute, evokes the familiar comfort and aroma of coffee. The warmth of ginger, roasted barley, chicory, and figs stimulates blood circulation and promotes energy and vitality.

1 cup water

1 (½-inch) piece fresh ginger, cut into slices

1 teaspoon instant herbal coffee substitute

1 tablespoon Almond Milk (page 34), Oat Milk (page 38), Rice Milk (34), or prepared vegan milk of your choice

1 teaspoon maple syrup or brown rice syrup

Pinch nutmeg

Bring the water and ginger to a boil in a small saucepan over medium-high heat. Decrease the heat. Simmer for 5 minutes. Strain the tea into a cup. Stir in the coffee substitute, Almond Milk, maple syrup, and nutmeg.

Almond Milk

Preparation Time: 10 minutes, plus overnight soak time
Yield: 4 (1-cup) servings

This recipe is easy—it only takes a bit of planning and a few extra minutes in the kitchen. Sweet and warming, almond milk helps pacify insomnia and anxiety, and is a wellness tonic for reproductive health.

---

1 cup whole raw almonds

8 cups water

1 teaspoon vanilla extract

Pinch salt

1 tablespoon maple syrup, coconut nectar, or raw agave nectar

Soak the almonds overnight (8 to 12 hours) in 4 cups of the water. Drain and rinse.

Put the almonds in a blender with 4 cups of fresh water. Process on high speed for 45 seconds, or until smooth. (You may need to do this in two batches if your blender won't hold all of the liquid.)

Strain the milk through a nut milk bag or double layer of cheesecloth into a large bowl or pitcher. Discard the pulp. Stir in the vanilla extract, salt, and maple syrup.

Note: Almond skins are astringent and tend to irritate the mucous membrane of the digestive tract, especially for vata types, who should peel off the almond skins after soaking.

Sweet Vanilla Almond Milk
(balances vata and pitta, increases kapha): Soak 2 pitted medjool dates in ½ cup of water for 5 minutes. Add the dates and the soak water to the almonds before blending.

Unsweetened Almond Milk
(balances vata, pitta, and kapha): Use ½ teaspoon of vanilla extract, and omit the maple syrup.

Rice Milk
(decreases vata, pitta, and kapha): Put 1 cup of cooked brown rice, 4 cups of water, 1 teaspoon of vanilla extract, 1 tablespoon of maple syrup, and a pinch of ground cardamom in a blender. Process until smooth.

Ginger–Turmeric Tea

decreases vata and kapha
increases pitta

Preparation Time: 15 minutes
Yield: 2 (1-cup) servings

Often called the "universal medicine," ginger is healing, warming, energizing, anti-inflammatory, and delicious. It stimulates appetite, improves circulation, and calms indigestion.

---

2 cups water

1 (2-inch) piece fresh ginger, peeled and grated

1 (2-inch) piece fresh turmeric root, peeled and grated

1 or 2 teaspoons raw yacon syrup or maple syrup

Bring the water, ginger, and turmeric to a boil in a medium saucepan. Decrease the heat. Simmer for 10 to 15 minutes. Strain the tea into cups. Stir in the yacon syrup to taste.

Note: Look for fresh turmeric root at natural food stores or Asian markets.

If fresh turmeric root is not available, substitute ½ teaspoon ground turmeric; add it with the yacon syrup.

Fresh Ginger Tea
(decreases vata and kapha, increases pitta): Bring 4 cups of water and 1 (2-inch) piece of fresh ginger, sliced (use 1 teaspoon ground ginger for pitta), to a boil in a medium saucepan. Boil for 1 minute. Remove from the heat. Let the tea steep for 10 to 15 minutes. Strain the tea into cups. Drink Fresh Ginger Tea at room temperature throughout the day for heart health, arthritis, sore throat, fatigue, indigestion, nausea, flatulence, fever, colds, cough, asthma, and laryngitis.

Feel Better Tea

Preparation Time: 15 minutes
Yield: 4 (1-cup) servings

Make this your tasty go-to tea when you're down and out with a cold, flu, or fatigue, and feel better fast.

---

4 cups water

1 (2-inch) piece fresh ginger, cut into thin slices

4 cloves garlic, minced

½ teaspoon cayenne

Juice of ½ lemon

1 to 2 teaspoons frozen apple juice concentrate or maple syrup (optional)

Bring the water and ginger to a boil in a large saucepan. Add the garlic. Cover. Decrease the heat. Simmer for 10 minutes. Remove from the heat. Stir in the cayenne. Strain the tea into cups. Stir in the lemon juice and optional juice concentrate to taste.

Feel Better Broth
(balances vata and pitta, decreases kapha): Substitute ground turmeric for the cayenne. Substitute 1 to 2 teaspoons of miso for the juice concentrate.

Mint-Lime Lemonade

Preparation Time: 30 minutes
Yield: 2 cups concentrate; 8 (1-cup) servings

This drink is delicious on a hot day, but try it gently warmed during evenings by the fire.

½ cup jaggery, dehydrated cane juice, or coconut sugar

1¼ cups water

1 teaspoon finely grated lemon zest

About 25 fresh mint leaves, or 3 large sprigs mint

⅓ cup freshly squeezed lime juice

¼ cup freshly squeezed lemon juice

Juice of 1 orange or tangerine

1 drop lavender essential oil (optional)

Pinch salt

1 slice lime, for garnish

Bring the jaggery, ½ cup of the water, and lemon zest to a boil in a medium saucepan over medium-high heat. Boil, stirring constantly, for 5 minutes. Remove the pan from the heat. Add the mint. Steep for 20 minutes. Remove and discard the mint.

Stir in the lime juice, lemon juice, orange juice, optional lavender essential oil, and salt. Let cool.

To make the lemonade, pour ¼ cup of the mint concentrate into a cup. Add the remaining ¾ cup of water and stir. Garnish with the lime slice if desired. Stored in a covered container in the refrigerator, Mint-Lime Lemonade will keep for 3 weeks.

India-Inspired Lemonade
(decreases vata, pitta, and kapha): There's a restaurant across the road from Gandhi's historical ashram in the Gujarati capital of Ahmedabad that serves the best lemon soda. This variation makes me think of it: Add 1 tablespoon of grated fresh ginger with the lemon zest. Omit the fresh mint (except for pitta) and lavender oil. Increase the lemon juice to ½ cup. Stir in ½ teaspoon of cayenne, 1 teaspoon of ground cardamom, and 1 pinch of ground ginger. Substitute ½ cup sparkling water for the ¾ cup of water. Garnish with a slice of lemon, if desired.

Oat Milk

Preparation Time: 10 minutes, plus overnight soak time
Yield: 4 (1-cup) servings

Oats are slippery and tend to have a laxative effect, which makes them especially good for vata. Great for building tissue, stabilizing blood sugar, reducing cholesterol, and calming the nervous system, Oat Milk is a versatile drink you can serve cold or warm.

1½ **cups rolled oats**

4 cups water

1 teaspoon vanilla extract

Pinch salt

1 tablespoon maple syrup or coconut nectar (optional)

Put the oats in a nut milk bag or a large muslin bag. Close the top so the oats will stay in the bag. Soak the oat bag overnight (8 to 12 hours) in the water in a large bowl or pitcher.

Hold the oat bag above the bowl to catch the oat milk as it streams out. Squeeze the oat bag until you've extracted all the oat milk you can. Discard the oats. Stir in the vanilla extract, salt, and optional maple syrup. Stored in a covered container in the refrigerator, Oat Milk will keep for 5 days.

Sole

Preparation Time: 24 hours
Yield: 2 cups

Sole (pronounced SO-lay) is a hydrating, mineral infusion that improves digestion, metabolism, and acid-alkaline balance. It is completely distinguishable from table salt, which has negative impacts on the body. I think Sole is a salt revolution!

---

2 cups water

2 tablespoons plus 2 teaspoons Himalayan pink salt or Celtic salt, plus more as needed

Pour the water and 2 tablespoons of the salt into a jar. Cover. Set aside overnight (8 to 12 hours). If all the salt crystals have dissolved by the next day and the water is clear, add another teaspoon of salt. Cover and set aside another night.

Repeat until no more salt will dissolve in the water and you see salt crystals at the bottom of the jar.

Stir 1 teaspoon of the Sole into 1 cup of fresh water every morning, or when you need a hydrating lift.

Note: The water and salt become ionized and create a therapeutic, pH-balanced, hydrating source of electrolytes. Salt is a natural antibacterial and fungicide, so you can safely add water and salt to the jar several times before starting over in a clean jar.

Steam and Bath Applications: Add 2 tablespoons of Sole to a steam inhalation or 1 cup or more to a bath. Both applications are detoxifying and anti-inflammatory, providing relief for inflamed respiratory conditions while positively affecting digestion and elimination.

Vegan Mango Lassi

Preparation Time: 5 minutes
Yield: 1 serving

SEE PHOTO FACING PAGE 25.

Coconut milk replaces creamy yogurt, and low-glycemic coconut sugar lends a nutritious source of sweetness to this traditional, tremendously healing Indian beverage.

¾ cup coconut milk

1 cup Oat Milk (page 38), Almond Milk (page 34), or prepared oat or almond milk

1 cup fresh or frozen mango chunks

2 tablespoons freshly squeezed lemon juice (about 1 lemon)

2 tablespoons coconut sugar or date sugar

Pinch ground cinnamon

1 teaspoon rejuvelac or powdered probiotic (optional)

Put the coconut milk, Oat Milk, mango, lemon juice, coconut sugar, cinnamon, and optional rejuvelac in a blender. Process until smooth, stopping occasionally to scrape down the blender jar. Sweeten with additional coconut sugar to taste.

Variation: Substitute unsulfured, unsweetened dried mango slices for the fresh or frozen mango. Soak the dried mango in enough water to cover for 30 minutes to 1 hour, or until very soft. Drain. (Vata and pitta may want to drink the soaking liquid.) Proceed with the recipe. Stored in a sealed container in the refrigerator, soaked, drained mango will keep for 1 week.

CHAPTER 7

Breakfast

BREAKFAST IS THE MOST IMPORTANT MEAL OF THE DAY, but not everyone relates to breakfast in quite the same way. Kapha types often skip breakfast or are satisfied with a piece of fruit before their hunger kicks in later in the day. While that's fine from time to time, a nourishing light breakfast is good for kapha and will also certainly ground excitable vata. Pitta types love to eat and will find the recipes here nourishing, satisfying, and filled with the protein they crave.

Superfoods are easily incorporated into a morning routine and give incredible energy to the mind, body, and spirit of all doshas.

Superfoods that Balance Vata
Sweetened acai, chia seeds, coconut butter, essential fatty acids, goji berries, lecithin powder, and maca root powder

Superfoods that Balance Pitta
Blue-green algae, chia seeds, flaxseeds, lecithin powder, spirulina, Vitamineral Green, and wheatgrass

Superfoods that Balance Kapha
Blue-green algae, raw cacao nibs, ground flaxseeds, fresh ginger, nopal cactus, probiotics, all spices, and spirulina

Ayurvedic Home Fries

balances vata, pitta, and kapha

Preparation Time: 25 minutes
Yield: 3 (1-cup) servings

SEE PHOTO FACING PAGE 89.

I used to love to go out for breakfast and order home-fried potatoes—until I found this recipe. Now I stay home and make my own because these are so yummy. Try these topped with Palmesan Cheese (page 90) or alongside a helping of Quinoa Pancakes (page 51).

½ cup water

2 red or purple potatoes, scrubbed and diced

1 teaspoon salt

1 teaspoon cumin seeds

½ teaspoon ground turmeric or mild curry powder

1 teaspoon dried rosemary

1 teaspoon dried basil or marjoram

3 collard green leaves, shredded

2 cloves garlic, minced (omit for pitta)

½ cup baby salad greens (optional)

1 tablespoon olive oil, for garnish

Bring the water to a boil in a heavy skillet over medium-high heat. Add the potatoes, salt, cumin, turmeric, rosemary, and basil. Decrease the heat to medium. Cook and stir for 5 minutes, or cover the skillet and let the potatoes cook for 5 minutes, stirring occasionally, to prevent them from sticking to the pan.

Stir in the collard greens and garlic. Cook just until the potatoes are soft, stirring often. Add 1 or more tablespoons of water as needed to prevent the potatoes from sticking to the pan. Serve over the optional salad greens. Drizzle each serving with oil, if desired.

Breakfast of *Chia*mpions

decreases vata, pitta, and kapha

Preparation Time: 10 minutes
Yield: 1 serving

Chia seeds are sattvic nutritional powerhouses. They provide hydration, fiber, and a gratifying crunch in this heavenly, nourishing breakfast porridge.

⅓ cup chia seeds

1 tablespoon goji berries

2½ tablespoons unsweetened shredded dried coconut or coconut flakes

½ cup Almond Milk (page 34), Oat Milk (page 38), prepared vegan milk of your choice, or coconut juice

1 tablespoon coconut sugar or date sugar

⅛ teaspoon ground cinnamon or ground cardamom

¼ cup blackberries, raspberries, or strawberries (optional)

1 teaspoon maca root powder (optional)

Combine the chia seeds, goji berries, and coconut in a small bowl. Add the Almond Milk. Set aside for 5 minutes. Stir in the coconut sugar, cinnamon, the optional berries and maca.

Creamy Coconut Kefir

decreases vata
balances pitta and kapha

Preparation Time: 10 minutes, plus 3 to 4 days fermentation time
Yield: 8 cups; 8 to 12 servings

I was skeptical about making vegan kefir until the first time I tasted it. It's better than you could ever imagine, especially when you spice it appropriately (and deliciously) for your dosha. The making of this recipe is a bit of an adventure, so bon voyage.

---

3 young coconuts

2 cups raw almonds

1 cup raw cashews

1 teaspoon ground cinnamon

1 teaspoon ground cardamom

1 packet vegan kefir starter

To make the coconut cream, place one coconut on its side. Use a sharp, heavy-duty knife to scrape and shave down the pointy top of the coconut to reveal the brownish, inner shell. Cut the top off the coconut by tapping around the circumference of the exposed inner shell with the square corner of the knife, creating a lid that comes right off.

Pour the coconut juice into a blender. Use a spoon to scrape out the coconut meat and put it in the blender. Repeat with the two remaining coconuts.

Put the almonds, cashews, cinnamon, and cardamom in the blender with the coconut. Process on high speed until creamy, stopping occasionally to scrape down the blender jar.

Pour the coconut mixture into a large saucepan. Cook over the lowest possible heat until it reaches 92 degrees F, or about body temperature. Use a candy thermometer to make sure the cream does not exceed 92 degrees F.

Remove from the heat. Stir in the kefir starter. Pour the mixture back into the blender. Process just until creamy. Pour the kefir into large, glass jars. Refrigerate for 3 to 4 days, or until the mixture becomes thick and sour, like yogurt. Stored in the refrigerator, Creamy Coconut Kefir will keep for about 5 days.

Variation: Garnish each serving with ½ cup soaked prunes or raisins and ⅛ teaspoon of cardamom for vata; ¼ cup chopped medjool dates or figs for pitta; or 1 tablespoon of grated fresh ginger and a pinch of cinnamon for kapha.

Favorite Coconut Kefir Breakfast

decreases vata and pitta
balances kapha

Preparation Time: 10 minutes
Yield: 1 serving

*It's important to regularly consume healthful strains of friendly bacteria, such as the **lactobacilli** found in vegan kefir and yogurt, and in this tasty, protein-rich, probiotic-friendly breakfast.*

1 cup Creamy Coconut Kefir (page 44) or prepared coconut yogurt

½ cup fresh blueberries, strawberries, or chopped fresh mango

2 tablespoons raw sunflower seeds, hempseeds, or raw pumpkin seeds

1 teaspoon frozen apple juice concentrate or brown rice syrup

⅛ teaspoon ground cardamom or ground nutmeg

2 tablespoons chopped fresh mint leaves

Mix all of the ingredients in a serving bowl.

Gentle Green Goodness

Preparation Time: 10 minutes
Yield: 2 to 4 servings

I learned of this fresh and heavenly drink from a truly beautiful man, beautiful, in part, because he drinks this every morning. Need I say more to inspire you to partake? Because of its high fiber content, this is a shake that you sip and chew.

½ **bunch dinosaur kale, roughly chopped**

4 stalks celery, cut into ½-inch pieces

1 (1-inch) piece fresh ginger, peeled and minced

2½ **tablespoons coconut butter**

1 tablespoon brown rice syrup or to taste

Pinch salt

1 cup water, plus more as needed

Juice of ½ lemon (optional)

Put the kale, celery, ginger, coconut butter, brown rice syrup, salt, and 1 cup of the water in a blender or food processor. Process until smooth, adding 1 or more tablespoons of water as needed to reach a smoothie-like consistency. Add the optional lemon juice. Process again until well combined.

Note: Gentle Green Goodness is a great "morning-after" drink to help your body recover from overconsumption of alcohol, sugar, processed foods, chocolate, table salt, or wheat.

Oat Groats Cereal

Preparation Time: 24 to 48 hours
Yield: 2 cups; 4 to 6 servings

Simple and tasty, oat groats contain little to no gluten and make a superb, raw breakfast cereal.

---

2 cups raw oat groats or buckwheat groats

8 cups water

1 cup Almond Milk (page 34) or prepared almond milk

½ cup strawberries, blueberries, or blackberries

1 (1-inch) piece fresh ginger, sliced thin (optional)

Raw agave nectar, molasses, or Jerusalem artichoke syrup

Soak the oat groats in the water in a large bowl for at least 24 hours. (The longer the groats soak, the softer they will become.) Drain and rinse well.

Serve ½ cup of the soaked groats with the Almond Milk, strawberries, the optional ginger, and agave nectar to taste. Stored in a sealed container in the refrigerator, Oat Groats Cereal will keep for 1 week.

Note: If your digestive system is sensitive to raw or cold foods, use the optional ginger. Add it to the groats and water, and soak for at least 48 hours.

Goddess Cereal
(balances vata and kapha, decreases pitta): Combine ½ cup of soaked oat groats, ¼ cup Goddess Trail Mix (page 142), and 1 cup of coconut juice for a simple, raw breakfast cereal.

Mineralizing Breakfast Broth balances vata, pitta, and kapha

Preparation Time: 10 minutes
Yield: 2 to 3 servings

This simple, speedy, fortifying broth strengthens and hydrates the body and spirit. It's rich in potassium and valuable trace minerals.

3 cups water

1 strip, square, or piece kombu

¼ teaspoon salt

½ small bulb fennel, chopped

2 stalks bok choy, chopped

1 tablespoon miso

Bring the water, kombu, salt, and fennel to a boil in a medium saucepan over medium-high heat. Decrease the heat to low. Add the bok choy. Simmer for 10 minutes. Remove from the heat. Stir in the miso until it dissolves. Serve as is, or pour the soup into a blender and process until smooth. Or, strain the soup for a delicious drink.

Breakfast Greens

Preparation Time: 10 minutes
Yield: 1 serving

Dark leafy greens are full of magnesium, a mineral that helps the body absorb calcium and promote relaxation and healthful sleep. I love to pair Breakfast Greens with Quinoa Pancakes (page 51). It also complements sweet, hot cereals.

2 tablespoons water

½ teaspoon ground cumin

½ teaspoon fennel seeds or
cumin seeds

½ bunch dinosaur kale, collard
greens, or spinach

1 (½-inch) piece fresh ginger, peeled
and minced

¼ cup toasted sea palm

1 tablespoon flaxseed oil or olive oil

1 teaspoon cider vinegar or ume
plum vinegar

1 teaspoon nutritional yeast flakes or
lecithin powder (optional)

¼ cup mung bean sprouts (optional)

Bring the water to a boil in a large, heavy skillet over medium-high heat. Add the cumin and fennel. Decrease the heat to medium. Stir in the kale, ginger, and sea palm. Cook and stir for 3 minutes, or until the kale is slightly wilted. To serve, top with the flaxseed oil, vinegar, and optional nutritional yeast and sprouts.

Quinoa Pancakes

Preparation Time: 20 minutes, plus overnight soak time
Yield: 8 to 10 pancakes; 5 servings

I love these pancakes. It's truly magical how effortless it is to turn this whole grain into scrumptious pancakes.

---

2 cups quinoa

4½ cups water

1 teaspoon salt

**1 to 2 tablespoons
coconut oil**

Soak the quinoa in 4 cups of the water in a large bowl for at least 8 hours at room temperature. Drain and rinse well.

Put the quinoa into a blender with the remaining ½ cup of water and the salt. (You may have to do this in batches.) Process until the mixture is the consistency of pancake batter, stopping occasionally to scrape down the blender jar. If the mixture is too thin, add another 2 tablespoons of the quinoa and process again. (A slightly thinner texture tends to cook more quickly.) If the mixture is too dry, add another 1 or 2 tablespoons of water and process again.

Melt 1 tablespoon of the coconut oil in a large skillet over medium heat. Pour about ¼ cup of the batter into the skillet to make one pancake. Cook for about 1½ minutes, or until the batter bubbles a little in the center and the edges turn golden brown. Turn the pancake and cook for another minute, or until it is golden brown on the second side. Add more coconut oil to the pan as needed. Stored in a covered container in the refrigerator, the remaining Quinoa Pancakes batter will keep for about 1 week.

Banana Chocolate-Chip Pancakes
(decreases vata, increases pitta, balances kapha): Stir in 1 ripe, mashed banana and ½ cup cacao nibs to the batter just before cooking. Serve with raw coconut nectar or maple syrup.

Blueberry Pancakes
(balances vata and pitta, decreases kapha): Stir in 1 cup fresh or frozen blueberries and ⅛ teaspoon ground cinnamon to the batter just before cooking.

Orange-Poppy Seed Pancakes
(decreases vata and kapha, increases pitta): Substitute ¼ cup orange juice for the water. Stir in ¼ cup poppy seeds and 1 teaspoon ground cardamom to the batter just before cooking.

Coconut-Mango Smoothie

Preparation Time: 5 minutes
Yield: 1 serving

Coconut juice, also called coconut water, is nature's sports drink: It's isotonic, meaning it contains the same electrolyte balance as human cells. Coconut juice was used during World War II for emergency blood transfusions on the battlefields.

---

1 mango, peeled, pitted, and chopped
  (2 mangoes for kapha)

1 banana, cut into 3 or 4 pieces
  (omit for kapha)

Juice of 2 oranges

1 cup coconut juice

⅛ teaspoon ground cinnamon

⅛ teaspoon cayenne (optional for
  vata and pitta)

Put all the ingredients in a blender. Process until smooth, stopping occasionally to scrape down the blender jar.

Note: If fresh mango is unavailable, see the Variation on page 40 for instructions for using dried mango.

Banana-Avocado Pudding

Preparation Time: 5 minutes
Yield: 1 serving

This surprisingly luscious treat would make as great a dessert as it does a light and hydrating breakfast.

1 ripe banana, cut into pieces

½ avocado

2 medjool dates, pitted

1 tablespoon water

1 heaping tablespoon raw, ground almonds (optional)

½ cup raspberries or strawberries (optional)

Put all the ingredients in a blender. Process for 30 seconds, or until smooth and creamy, stopping occasionally to scrape down the blender jar.

Hot Amaranth Porridge

decreases vata and kapha
increases pitta

Preparation Time: 30 minutes
Yield: 2 to 4 servings

Amaranth is a warming alternative to oatmeal, especially on cool winter mornings. Rotate this recipe into your regular breakfast routine; it's a great source of gluten-free fiber and protein, and it tastes delicious.

1 cup amaranth

1 teaspoon ground cinnamon

2 cups water

4 dried figs, chopped

¼ cup raisins

3 tablespoons flaxseeds, chia seeds, or raw sunflower seeds

Molasses or maple syrup to taste

Pour the amaranth into a medium, heavy saucepan over medium heat. Stir in the cinnamon. Toast for 30 seconds, stirring often. Add the water, figs, and raisins. Bring to a boil. Decrease the heat. Simmer for 15 to 20 minutes, stirring occasionally, until the water has been absorbed. Sprinkle with the flaxseeds and serve with the molasses.

Savory Spiced Amaranth
(decreases vata and kapha, balances pitta): Versatile and delicious, amaranth porridge doubles as a savory grain dish. Substitute ground turmeric for the cinnamon, add 1 teaspoon of salt, and substitute 2 teaspoons of minced fresh ginger for the figs and raisins. Omit the molasses, and stir in a handful of chopped fresh basil before serving.

54 CHAPTER 7

Morning Cupcakes

Preparation Time: 1 hour, 10 minutes
Yield: 16 to 18 cupcakes

These sweet and savory veggie-laden cakes are well worth the time it takes to make them.

1 cup amaranth flour or quinoa flour

1½ cups brown rice flour or sorghum flour

½ cup coconut flour

1 tablespoon tapioca flour

¼ cup almond meal

2 teaspoons baking powder

1 teaspoon salt

½ teaspoon xanthan gum (optional)

¼ cup coconut oil

½ cup millet

1 tablespoon ground cinnamon

1 teaspoon ground nutmeg or ground cumin

1 tablespoon dried basil

1 tablespoon caraway seeds or fennel seeds

1 cup grated zucchini

¼ cup grated carrots

1 or 2 tablespoons chopped fresh dill, cilantro, or parsley

½ cup raisins or unsweetened dried cranberries

1 cup mashed, ripe banana (about 2 medium bananas)

2 cups apple juice, pear juice, or coconut–pineapple juice

½ cup raw cane sugar, date sugar, or dehydrated cane juice

⅓ cup raw sunflower seeds

1 cup softened coconut butter

Preheat the oven to 375 degrees F. Line a muffin pan with paper muffin cups or oil the muffin pan with coconut oil.

Combine the flours, almond meal, baking powder, salt, and the optional xanthan gum in a medium bowl and set aside. To melt the coconut oil, place the container on the warm stovetop for a few minutes, or in a bowl of hot water for 1 minute.

Mix the millet, cinnamon, nutmeg, basil, caraway seeds, zucchini, carrots, dill, and raisins in a large bowl. Beat the oil, banana, apple juice, and sugar in a medium bowl. Add the banana mixture to the millet mixture and stir until well combined. Mix in the sunflower seeds. Add the flour mixture and combine.

The cupcakes will not rise, so fill each muffin cup with batter and use a spoon to round the tops. Bake for 30 to 35 minutes, or until a toothpick inserted in the centers comes out clean. Spread 1 tablespoon of the softened coconut butter on each muffin before serving.

Note: Substitute 3¼ cups of gluten-free baking mix (available at most natural food stores and supermarkets) for the flours and the almond meal.

CHAPTER 8

Salads and Salad Dressings

LIGHT, CRUNCHY, AND FULL OF FIBER, salads are colorful, beautiful additions to most meals. Vata does best with salads that are well oiled and adorned with nuts and seeds. The cool crunch of crisp lettuce, kale, and collards helps pitta types feel great, and kapha thrives on light, leafy green vegetables, combined with additions such as shredded carrots and spicy sprouts.

Not all oils are created equal, so make a habit of using oils that are best suited for your constitution. Always choose raw, unfiltered, expeller- or cold-pressed oils of the highest quality.

Oils that Balance Vata
Avocado, borage, evening primrose, grapeseed, hempseed, olive, pumpkin seed, sunflower, and sesame

Oils that Balance Pitta
Avocado, borage, coconut, flaxseed, hempseed, and olive

Oils that Balance Kapha
Coconut, flaxseed, grapeseed, hempseed, and sunflower

Sea Vegetable Salad

balances vata
decreases pitta and kapha

Preparation Time: 15 minutes
Yield: 4 servings

This recipe is hydrating and mineralizing and is a good salad for vata and pitta. The longer this salad marinates, the yummier it becomes.

2 cups raw, dried sea vegetables

4 cups water

4 cups minced red or green cabbage (use baby salad greens for vata)

2 green onions, minced

1 small daikon radish, or 4 large red radishes, grated

1 small jicama, peeled and diced

1 (2-inch) piece fresh ginger, peeled and minced

¼ cup raw sesame seeds

¼ cup slivered raw almonds or raw cashew pieces

2 tablespoons cider vinegar or coconut vinegar

2 tablespoons olive oil

¼ cup freshly squeezed orange juice (about 2 oranges)

1 tablespoon miso

½ teaspoon salt

2 cups baby salad greens (optional)

Soak the sea vegetables in the water in a large bowl. Set aside.

Toss the cabbage, onions, daikon, jicama, ginger, sesame seeds, and almonds in a separate large bowl.

In a small bowl, whisk the vinegar, oil, orange juice, miso, and salt until the miso has dissolved. (If the miso does not dissolve easily, add 1 tablespoon of hot water.)

Drain the sea vegetables. Coarsely chop into 1- or 2-inch pieces. Add them to the cabbage mixture. Pour the dressing over the cabbage mixture. Toss well. Serve over the optional greens. Stored in a covered container in the refrigerator, Sea Vegetable Salad will keep for about 5 days

Quinoa Salad with Apricot, Lime, and Ginger

balances vata, pitta, and kapha

Preparation Time: 45 minutes
Yield: 4 to 6 servings

Pronounced KEEN-wah, this gluten-free grain has won over health-conscious Westerners with its fast cooking time (almost half the time of most rice), high protein content, nutrient density, and purifying qualities. When cooked, it is light, fluffy, and warming, with a delicate crunch that is especially good for kapha.

Quinoa

1 cup quinoa

2 cups water

1 teaspoon cumin seeds

2 teaspoons ground cumin

½ teaspoon ground turmeric

1 teaspoon salt

Dressing

Zest of 2 limes

2 tablespoons freshly squeezed lime juice

Juice of ½ orange

4 green onions, minced

1 (2-inch) piece fresh ginger, peeled and minced

1 small jalapeño chile, seeded and minced (omit for pitta)

1 teaspoon ground coriander

1 teaspoon ground cardamom

To make the quinoa, pour it into a fine-mesh strainer. Rinse and drain several times under cold running water. (This removes naturally occurring *saponin*, a plant steroid that forms a soapy, protective coating over quinoa.)

Bring the quinoa and water to a boil in a large saucepan over medium-high heat. Decrease the heat to simmer. Add the cumin seeds, ground cumin, turmeric, and salt. Simmer for about 15 minutes, or until the water is absorbed and the germ has separated and curled around the quinoa. Remove from the heat. Cover. Let cool for a few minutes.

To make the dressing, whisk all the dressing ingredients in a large bowl. In a separate small bowl, combine all the additions.

Transfer the cooled quinoa to the bowl with the dressing. Toss well. Stir in the additions.

1 teaspoon fennel seeds

½ teaspoon ground mustard

⅓ cup olive oil

1 tablespoon ume plum vinegar
  or cider vinegar

1 teaspoon salt

Additions

6 dried apricots (preferably Turkish),
  minced

¼ cup unsweetened dried
  cranberries, or raisins

3 tablespoons chopped crystallized
  ginger, or currants

½ cup slivered almonds or raw
  pine nuts

1 teaspoon ground cinnamon

⅛ teaspoon ground nutmeg

1 cup chopped fresh dill weed,
  cilantro, or basil

Variations: Add 2 tablespoons of olive oil for an especially moist dish. Substitute any combination of chopped dried pineapple, prunes, pears, cherries, walnuts, sesame seeds, or hempseeds for the apricots, cranberries, and almonds in the Additions.

Luscious Lemon Dressing

decreases vata, pitta, and kapha

Preparation Time: 15 minutes
Yield: About 1½ cups

This dressing is so good it may never make it to your salad. But in case it does, try it over a bed of lettuce with steamed sweet potatoes, slivered almonds, and sprouts. Or pour it over Herbed Millet (page 137) for a savory, grounding meal.

1 cup raw tahini or cashew butter

½ cup water or olive oil

Juice of 2 lemons

1 tablespoon cider vinegar

1 (1-inch) piece fresh ginger, peeled and minced

¼ cup chopped fresh cilantro

1 teaspoon ground coriander

1 teaspoon ground cumin

1 teaspoon fennel seeds

2 teaspoons salt

1 teaspoon ground black pepper

Put all the ingredients in a blender or food processor. Process until smooth, stopping occasionally to scrape down the blender jar or work bowl. Stored in a covered container in the refrigerator, Luscious Lemon Dressing will keep for 7 days. Shake well before each use.

Faux French Dressing

Preparation Time: 10 minutes
Yield: About 1 cup

Tangy and spirited, this dressing plays an integral role in the Big Tempeh Mac (page 105), my slow-food version of a famous fast-food sandwich. Faux French Dressing also is delicious over a bed of crisp romaine lettuce and Baked Tempeh (page 126).

½ **cup olive oil or grapeseed oil**

2 **tablespoons cider vinegar or coconut vinegar**

2 **tablespoons freshly squeezed lemon juice**

2 **teaspoons raw agave nectar or maple syrup**

½ **teaspoon salt**

1 **teaspoon ground coriander**

½ **teaspoon ground mustard**

½ **teaspoon paprika (optional)**

⅛ **teaspoon cayenne**

2 **cups chopped fresh cilantro**

½ **avocado (optional)**

Put all the ingredients in a blender or food processor. Process until smooth. Stored in a covered container in the refrigerator, Faux French Dressing will keep for 4 days. Shake well before each use.

Kale Summer Salad

Preparation Time: 15 minutes
Yield: 4 to 6 servings

People who have never tried it are surprised to hear that raw kale is not only edible, but it also tastes great and is easy to prepare. As the queen of my kitchen, I lift my dark leafy green "sword" to the sky and declare, "May everyone love kale."

---

1 bunch dinosaur kale, minced

2 teaspoons salt

½ cup slivered almonds

½ cup raw pumpkin seeds

1 small red onion, minced (omit for vata and pitta)

1½ avocados, diced

1 cup mung bean sprouts or sunflower sprouts

Juice of 2 lemons

¼ cup olive oil

1 tablespoon cider vinegar or ume plum vinegar

2 tablespoons unsweetened shredded coconut (optional)

1 tablespoon fennel seeds

1 teaspoon ground coriander

Put the kale in a large bowl. Sprinkle with the salt. With your hands, massage the salt into the kale for about 30 seconds, using a constant kneading motion. (Massaging the kale softens it and makes it tender.)

Add the almonds, pumpkin seeds, onion, avocados, sprouts, lemon juice, oil, vinegar, optional coconut, fennel, and coriander. Toss well. Serve immediately. Stored without the sprouts in a covered container in the refrigerator, Kale Summer Salad will keep for 5 days.

Note: Vata may prefer to let the salad marinate for 1 to 2 hours before serving to soften the kale further.

Baby Green Bean Salad

Preparation Time: 15 minutes
Yield: 2 to 3 servings

I love this salad because it's quick yet so diverse. Everyone thinks you spent a long time making it. It's a really simple mix of great flavors and texture.

½ cup raisins

1 cup hot water

4 cups baby salad greens

2 cups cooked red kidney beans
  or chickpeas

1 avocado, diced

½ cup sunflower sprouts

¼ cup raw sunflower seeds

¼ teaspoon salt

½ teaspoon dried rosemary

½ cup Vegan Paneer Cheese
  (page 134) (optional)

1 small beet, shredded (optional)

½ cup sprouted lentils (optional)

Talya's Kitchen House Vinaigrette
  (page 68)

Soak the raisins in a small bowl of hot water while you prepare the salad.

Put the greens, beans, avocado, sunflower sprouts, sunflower seeds, salt, rosemary, optional Vegan Paneer Cheese, beet, and lentils in a large bowl. Drain the raisins and add them to the salad. Toss well. Serve with Talya's Kitchen House Vinaigrette.

Super-Electrolyte Salad

Preparation Time: 15 minutes
Yield: 6 cups; 4 to 6 servings

Green vegetables contain magnesium, and white vegetables contain potassium. Add a little good-quality salt, and you've got the makings for a salad that nourishes, hydrates, and energizes the whole body.

½ **bunch bok choy, minced**

½ **bunch dinosaur kale, minced**

1 small jicama, peeled and diced

1 cup minced fresh cilantro leaves

1 avocado, diced

1 cup sunflower sprouts or
mung bean sprouts

1 cup soaked, drained, slivered
raw almonds or pine nuts

2 teaspoons salt

1 teaspoon ground fennel or
fennel seeds

½ **cup sunflower oil or olive oil**

¼ **cup cider vinegar or**
coconut vinegar

Combine all the ingredients in a large bowl. Toss well.

Purple Potato Salad

Preparation Time: 20 minutes
Yield: 2 to 4 servings

Not only is the purple potato gorgeous and less starchy than its white-fleshed cousins, but its purple pigment also indicates a boost of health-enhancing antioxidants that help your heart, immune system, and memory. Enjoy Purple Potato Salad's stunning color next to the Carrot-Raisin Salad (page 67) for a real rainbow of a meal.

---

6 purple potatoes, scrubbed and cut into ½-inch cubes (about 3 cups)

2 tablespoons Vegan Mayonnaise (page 75) or prepared vegan mayonnaise

2 teaspoons stone-ground mustard

2 tablespoons cider vinegar

1 tablespoon olive oil

½ teaspoon dried dill weed

1 teaspoon ground cumin

½ teaspoon ground black pepper (omit for pitta)

½ cup toasted sea palm

½ cup raw pumpkin seeds

¼ cup chopped fresh cilantro

Place a steamer basket in a saucepan with about ½ cup of water. Bring the water to a boil. Put the potatoes in the steamer basket. Cover. Steam for 8 minutes, or until fork-tender.

Meanwhile, whisk the Vegan Mayonnaise, mustard, vinegar, oil, dill, cumin, and pepper in a large bowl.

Drain the potatoes and transfer them to the bowl with the dressing. Toss well. Stir in the sea palm, pumpkin seeds, and cilantro. Serve immediately.

Fresh Red Onion Coleslaw

Preparation Time: 20 minutes
Yield: About 3 cups

A perfect salad for kapha, this colorful coleslaw is like the gift that keeps on giving. Its flavors will mellow and get better for days after you make it.

---

2 cups minced green cabbage

1 cup minced red cabbage

1 small leek, minced

1 small red onion, minced

1 tablespoon cider vinegar or
brown rice vinegar

1 tablespoon dill weed

½ teaspoon salt

½ teaspoon ground black pepper
(omit for pitta)

1 tablespoon frozen apple juice
concentrate, or 2 tablespoons
apple juice

¼ cup Vegan Mayonnaise (page 75)
or prepared vegan mayonnaise

½ cup raw sunflower seeds (optional)

½ cup chopped fresh cilantro or
basil leaves (optional)

Combine the green and red cabbage, leek, and onion in a large bowl. Whisk the vinegar, dill, salt, pepper, juice concentrate, and Vegan Mayonnaise in a medium bowl. Pour the dressing over the cabbage mixture and toss well. Marinate for 1 hour. Just before serving, stir in the sunflower seeds and cilantro. Stored in a covered container in the refrigerator, Fresh Red Onion Coleslaw will keep for 1 week.

Carrot-Raisin Salad

decreases vata and pitta
increases kapha

Preparation Time: 15 minutes
Yield: 4 (1-cup) servings

This recipe was inspired by a jaunt through one of my favorite natural food stores to find something fresh and grounding after some good shopping. It's scrumptious on its own or as a complement to Ayurvedic Brown Rice (page 128).

⅔ cup raisins

1 cup hot water

2 cups grated carrots

1 cup grated zucchini

4 green onions, minced
(omit for vata and pitta)

2 tablespoons sesame seeds

¼ cup Vegan Mayonnaise (page 75)
or prepared vegan mayonnaise

1 tablespoon toasted or regular
sesame oil, or sunflower oil

1 tablespoon brown rice syrup or
coconut nectar

Juice of 1 orange

1 teaspoon curry powder

1 teaspoon caraway seeds or
cumin seeds

¼ teaspoon salt

Soak the raisins in a small bowl of hot water while you prepare the salad. Combine the carrots, zucchini, onions, and sesame seeds in a large bowl.

In a separate bowl, combine the Vegan Mayonnaise with the oil, brown rice syrup, orange juice, curry powder, caraway seeds, and salt. Pour the dressing over the carrot mixture. Drain the raisins and add them to the salad. Mix well.

Note: Vata can enjoy the sweet and grounding benefits of the raisin soak water. Pour it into a glass when draining the raisins.

Talya's Kitchen House Vinaigrette

Preparation Time: 35 minutes
Yield: ½ cup

This has been the house dressing at Talya's Kitchen for years. Simple, refreshing, satisfying, and delicious, this dressing boasts essential fatty acids and digestive-regulating spices.

¼ cup olive oil

2 tablespoons cider vinegar or ume plum vinegar

Juice of 1 lime or lemon

1 tablespoon fennel seeds

1 teaspoon ground coriander

½ teaspoon salt

Put all the ingredients in a glass jar with a tight-fitting lid. Shake well. Set aside for 30 minutes to allow the flavors to develop. Shake well before each use.

Note: For kapha, substitute sunflower oil for the olive oil. Use lemon juice instead of lime juice. For pitta, replace 2 tablespoons of the olive oil with hempseed oil.

Vegan Caesar Salad

Preparation Time: 30 minutes
Yield: 2 servings

It's just as good as the real thing, maybe even better. My family freaks out (in a really good way) when I make it.

Croutons

2 teaspoons coconut oil

2 slices brown rice bread or sprouted grain bread

2 cloves garlic, minced

Salad

½ head romaine lettuce, cut into 1-inch strips

1 small red onion, sliced thin (omit for pitta)

2 tablespoons Palmesan Cheese (page 90) or prepared vegan Parmesan (optional)

2 tablespoons Vegan Caesar Dressing (page 70)

1 teaspoon ground coriander

1 teaspoon ground black pepper

Preheat the oven to 375 degrees F. To make the croutons, spread the coconut oil on the bread slices. Sprinkle the garlic on each slice. Place the bread slices on a small baking sheet. Toast for 5 to 7 minutes, or until golden brown and crisp. Cut into ¼-inch cubes. Set aside.

Put the lettuce and onion in a large bowl. Add the Palmesan Cheese, Vegan Caesar Dressing, coriander, and pepper. Toss well. Sprinkle with the croutons.

Vegan Caesar Dressing

Preparation Time: 10 minutes
Yield: ½ cup

This is the signature dressing for the Vegan Caesar Salad, of course. But don't be surprised if you start adding it to steamed vegetables, over whole grains, or as a dip with fresh radishes, celery, and apples.

1 tablespoon miso

½ cup hot water

½ cup raw cashews or pine nuts

1 tablespoon coconut vinegar or
   cider vinegar

1 teaspoon stone-ground mustard

2 cloves garlic, minced
   (omit for pitta)

Juice of 1 lemon

1 teaspoon dried thyme or basil

Combine the miso with the hot water in a small bowl until the miso has dissolved. Put all of the remaining ingredients in a blender or a food processor. Process until smooth and creamy. Add the miso mixture. Process until well blended. Stored in a covered container in the refrigerator, Vegan Caesar Dressing will keep for 5 days. Shake well before each use.

Tahini–Miso Dressing

Preparation time: 10 minutes
Yield: 1¼ cups

Deep and rich with a sweet and sour punch, this alkalizing, nutrition-packed dressing tastes divine over Zucchini Pasta (page 102) and cool, crunchy salads.

---

3 tablespoons miso

⅓ cup hot water

¼ cup freshly squeezed lemon juice

⅓ cup raw tahini

¼ cup olive oil, plus more as needed for consistency

1 teaspoon tamari, Bragg Liquid Aminos or coconut aminos

1 tablespoon maple syrup or raw agave nectar

½ teaspoon ground cumin

¼ teaspoon garlic powder

¼ teaspoon onion powder

Put the miso and water in a blender or food processor. Process for 10 seconds, or until well mixed. Add the lemon juice, tahini, ¼ cup of the olive oil, tamari, maple syrup, cumin, garlic powder, and onion powder. Process until smooth. Add 1 or more tablespoons of the olive oil. Process until the dressing reaches the desired consistency. Stored in a covered container in the refrigerator, Tahini-Miso Dressing will keep for 5 days. Shake well before each use.

Creamy Cucumber-Tahini Dressing

Preparation Time: 15 minutes

Yield: 2 cups

SEE PHOTO FACING PAGE 120.

Simple and easy to make, this is a refreshing dressing for summer salads.

1 cucumber, sliced in half lengthwise, seeded and chopped

¼ cup raw tahini

¼ cup olive oil

Juice of 1 lemon

½ teaspoon salt

1 clove garlic, minced (omit for pitta)

2 tablespoons minced red onion (omit for vata and pitta)

1 teaspoon ground coriander

Put all the ingredients in a blender or food processor. Process until smooth and creamy, stopping occasionally to scrape down the blender jar or work bowl. Stored in a covered container in the refrigerator, Creamy Cucumber-Tahini Dressing will keep for 3 days. Shake well before each use.

CHAPTER 9

Sauces, Spreads and Condiments

A BALANCING AYURVEDIC PRACTICE IS TO INCLUDE ALL SIX RASAS, or tastes, at each meal. Even if you are someone who thrives on sweet and sour flavors, dashes of bitter, astringent, salty, and pungent foods in your diet can help keep the doshas in harmony.

The tantalizing recipes in this section are helpful tools for balancing diets for your entire family, even when they have different dominant constitutions. Adding a sauce, beginning a meal with a spread, serving condiments on the side, or garnishing a dish with fresh herbs and sprouts are easy ways to balance meals.

In vegan ayurveda, high-protein sources are mostly limited to the legume world, which makes beans a staple. High in fiber, low in fat, and highly nutritious, beans can work well for your body; the key is learning which ones support you. The recipes featuring legumes also include spices and sea vegetables that can assist your body in digesting beans easily.

Raw nuts and seeds are another common base in many of these sauces, spreads, and condiments. They are excellent protein-rich alternatives to dairy products. Most people won't even know these dishes are vegan until you, well, spill the beans.

Nuts and Seeds that Balance Vata
Skinless almonds, cashews, Brazil nuts, chia, coconut, whole flaxseeds, pine nuts, pumpkin seeds, sesame seeds, sprouted peanuts, and sunflower seeds

Nuts and Seeds that Balance Pitta
Soaked almonds, chia, coconut, flaxseeds, hempseeds, and sunflower seeds

Nuts and Seeds that Balance Kapha
Almonds, chia, dried coconut, ground flaxseeds, hempseeds, poppy seeds, pumpkin seeds, and sunflower seeds

Amazing Pesto Chutney

balances vata, pitta, and kapha

Preparation Time: 15 minutes
Yield: About 4 cups

SEE PHOTO FACING PAGE 121.

Meet the queen of condiments. Packed with nutritious greens, enzymes, protein, essential fatty acids, and hydrating minerals, this pesto will be your new go-to addition to almost any meal. It freezes well and, stored in a tightly covered container in the refrigerator, will keep for 3 weeks.

½ cup raw tahini or almond butter

½ cup toasted sea palm or raw, wild nori

Juice of 1 lemon

1 cup olive oil, plus more as needed for desired consistency

1 bunch cilantro, chopped

1 bunch dill weed, chopped

1 bulb fennel, chopped

2 teaspoons ground cumin

1 teaspoon ground coriander

1 teaspoon salt

½ teaspoon ground pepper (omit for pitta)

Put the tahini, sea palm, lemon juice, and ½ cup of the olive oil in a food processor or blender. Process for 5 to 10 seconds. Add half each of the cilantro, dill, and fennel. Process for another 20 seconds. Add the remaining ½ cup of olive oil, the remaining cilantro, dill, and fennel, the cumin, coriander, salt, and pepper. Process for another 2 minutes, or until smooth and creamy, stopping occasionally to scrape down the work bowl or blender jar. If the pesto is too thick, add another 1 to 2 tablespoons of olive oil and process again.

Note: It's admittedly difficult to measure ½ cup of sea vegetables perfectly. Pack some into a measuring cup, and do your best to estimate.

Vegan Mayonnaise

balances vata, pitta, and kapha

Preparation Time: 15 minutes
Yield: 1 cup

While it's fine to use the store-bought version, it's much more fun to make mayonnaise yourself. You might be surprised at how easy it is.

¼ cup ground almonds, cashews, Brazil nuts, macadamia nuts, or pine nuts

1 teaspoon dry mustard

¼ teaspoon ground cumin

¼ teaspoon ground coriander

⅛ teaspoon cayenne (omit for pitta)

2 tablespoons freshly squeezed lemon juice

2 teaspoons cider vinegar or brown rice vinegar

2 tablespoons plus 2 teaspoons Almond Milk (page 34), Oat Milk (page 38), or prepared almond or oat milk

1 teaspoon salt

½ teaspoon ground pepper

½ cup olive oil

Put the almonds, mustard, cumin, coriander, cayenne, lemon juice, vinegar, Almond Milk, salt, and pepper in a blender. Process until well combined, stopping occasionally to scrape down the blender jar.

With the blender running, add ¼ cup of the oil a few drops at a time. Add the remaining ¼ cup oil in a fine, steady stream until the mixture is creamy. Stored in a covered glass jar in the refrigerator, Vegan Mayonnaise will keep for 3 to 5 days.

Note: This will yield a thinner mayonnaise than one made with eggs. It will thicken up some in the refrigerator.

Tridoshic Spice Mix

balances vata, pitta, and kapha

Preparation Time: 5 minutes
Yield: ¾ cup

Fennel seeds, cumin seeds, and coriander seeds are digestive aids that balance all three doshas. This spice mix promotes digestion while offering gentle warmth and flavor to any meal.

¼ **cup fennel seeds**

¼ **cup cumin seeds**
   or ground cumin

¼ **cup ground coriander**

Combine all the ingredients in a small bowl. Stored in a glass jar at room temperature, Tridoshic Spice Mix will keep for 6 months.

Gomasio

Preparation Time: 10 minutes
Yield: 1½ cups

Gomasio is a traditional macrobiotic condiment often used as a healthful substitute for salt. Sprinkle it over Macrobiotic Brown Rice (page 97), steamed vegetables, and salads. Rich in calcium and minerals, it brings fantastic flavor to the table.

1 cup raw sesame seeds

½ cup raw sunflower seeds

½ cup toasted sea palm

1 tablespoon ground cumin

2 teaspoons dried nettles (optional)

1 teaspoon ground coriander

1 teaspoon salt

½ teaspoon ground pepper

Place a large, heavy skillet over medium heat. Spread the sesame seeds in a single layer in the skillet. Cook 3 to 4 minutes, stirring constantly, or until the seeds become aromatic and start to pop. Immediately remove from the heat.

Put the sesame seeds and all of the remaining ingredients in a food processor or blender. Process until the seeds are ground and all the ingredients are well combined.

Note: Sesame seeds are tiny, sattvic protein sources rich in oils and minerals that strengthen the bones and act as a rejuvenative tonic for vata. For a highly nutritive food for the kidneys and adrenal glands, substitute black sesame seeds for the brown ones.

Goddess of Artichoke Dip

decreases vata and pitta
balances kapha

Preparation Time: 1 hour
Yield: 6 to 8 servings

This delicious dip was created in honor of a lovely woman I know who was having a birthday party. It seems like a lot of work in print, but most of the time is devoted to steaming the artichokes. Make it when artichokes are in season.

5 medium to large artichokes

2 lemons, cut in half

½ cup Vegan Mayonnaise (page 75) or prepared vegan mayonnaise

1 tablespoon grated lemon zest

Juice of 1 lime

1 bunch spinach leaves, chopped

1 teaspoon dried thyme

1 teaspoon dried basil

2 tablespoons olive oil

½ teaspoon salt

½ teaspoon ground pepper

Remove the stems and tips of the outer leaves of the artichokes with a sharp knife. Squeeze the lemon halves over the artichokes and set aside.

Place a steamer basket in a large pot with 2 inches of water. Bring the water to a boil. Decrease the heat to medium. Place the artichokes upside-down in the steamer basket. (You may need to steam the artichokes in batches if they are particularly large.) Cover. Steam for 25 minutes, or until the bottoms of the artichokes are fork-tender and a leaf near the center pulls out easily. Add hot water to the pot if the water level drops too low.

Let the artichokes cool for 20 to 30 minutes. Pull off all the leaves and set them aside. Use a spoon to scrape off the chokes (the fuzzy parts of the heart) and remove the hearts. Put the hearts, Vegan Mayonnaise, lemon zest, lime juice, spinach, thyme, basil, oil, salt, and pepper in a food processor. Process until smooth and creamy, stopping occasionally to scrape down the work bowl. If the mixture is too thick, add another 1 or 2 tablespoons of olive oil. Season with additional salt to taste.

To serve, transfer the dip to a small bowl. Place the bowl on a large plate. Surround the bowl with the reserved artichoke leaves.

Indian-Spiced Guacamole

Preparation Time: 10 minutes
Yield: 1 cup

Definitely not your traditional guacamole, but even diehard fans of the salsa-laden variety take pleasure and surprise in how much they like this exotic version. It's a lovely accompaniment to Indian and festive meals.

2 large avocados

1 tablespoon olive oil

Juice of ½ lime

1½ teaspoons salt

¼ cup chopped fresh basil

1 teaspoon ground cumin

1 teaspoon ground coriander

½ teaspoon ground cardamom

½ teaspoon ground cinnamon (use ¼ teaspoon for pitta)

½ teaspoon ground pepper (use ¼ teaspoon for pitta)

¼ teaspoon cayenne (omit for pitta)

1 teaspoon brown mustard seeds (optional)

½ teaspoon caraway seeds (optional)

Mash the avocado in a medium bowl with a fork or potato masher until creamy. Mix in all of the remaining ingredients.

Fresh Mango Ketchup

decreases vata
balances pitta and kapha

Preparation time: 10 minutes
Yield: 1 cup

As a child, ketchup was my favorite food. I ate it on absolutely everything, including carrots and applesauce. This tangy, sweet, creamy version can be devoured on anything you would usually dip, douse, or drizzle with ketchup.

1 cup peeled and chopped fresh mango, or 1 cup soaked, dried mango (see Note page 40)

¼ cup chopped sun-dried tomatoes

2 tablespoons raw agave nectar or maple syrup

3 tablespoons sunflower oil or olive oil

1 tablespoon cider vinegar or coconut vinegar

½ teaspoon ground ginger (omit for pitta)

¼ teaspoon salt

¼ teaspoon ground cloves

¼ teaspoon ground coriander

¼ teaspoon ground cardamom

⅛ teaspoon ground cinnamon

Pinch cayenne (omit for pitta)

Put all the ingredients in a blender or food processor. Process about 20 seconds, or until well blended, stopping occasionally to scrape down the blender jar or work bowl. The ketchup should be smooth, thick, and luscious. If the ketchup is too thick, add another tablespoon of oil and process again.

Stored in a covered container in the refrigerator, Fresh Mango Ketchup will keep for 1 week.

Fresh Mango Mustard
(decreases vata, balances pitta and kapha): Omit the sun-dried tomatoes and 1 tablespoon of the sunflower oil. Add a pinch of ground black pepper.

Garlic Dream Sauce

balances vata and kapha
increases pitta

Preparation Time: 15 minutes
Yield: About 2 cups

Cashew cream replaces heavy cream in this outstanding sauce that features garlic's powerful antiviral, antifungal, and antibacterial properties. Use it as a creamy ranch-like salad dressing or dip, or as a pasta cream sauce. It's appetizing over pretty much anything, as long as you are a garlic lover.

---

1 cup raw cashews

1½ cups very cold water

1 tablespoon miso

2 tablespoons hot water

1 tablespoon freshly squeezed
    lemon juice

½ teaspoon salt

½ teaspoon ground coriander

¼ teaspoon ground pepper

1 teaspoon dried dill weed

1½ tablespoons minced garlic

Put the cashews and the cold water in a blender. Process on high speed for 3 minutes, or until smooth and the consistency of heavy cream, stopping occasionally to scrape down the blender jar. Set aside.

Combine the miso with the hot water in a medium bowl until the miso has dissolved. Stir in the lemon juice, salt, coriander, pepper, and dill. Add the cashew cream and garlic and mix well.

Note: Garlic Dream Sauce will thicken as it cools, so if the sauce seems thin, refrigerate it for 1 hour. If it is still too thin, return it to the blender, and add ¼ cup raw cashews. Process until smooth and creamy.

Brazil Nut Garlic Dream Sauce
(decreases vata, increases pitta and kapha): Substitute Brazil nuts for the cashews. Soak them in water for at least 1 hour before using. The texture won't be quite as smooth, but the taste will be exquisite.

Cooked Garlic Dream Sauce
(balances vata, pitta, and kapha): Melt 1 teaspoon of coconut oil in a medium saucepan over medium-low heat. Add the garlic. Cook and stir for 1 minute. Proceed with the rest of the recipe. Pour the sauce into the saucepan with the garlic. Heat the sauce for 1 or 2 minutes over very low heat.

Raw Sauerkraut

Preparation time: 45 minutes, plus 7 to 10 days fermentation time
Yield: About 4 quarts

Raw Sauerkraut provides natural probiotics and tastes incredibly good, if I do say so myself. Sauerkraut must be raw to impart health benefits. Try a tablespoon on whole grain dishes, soups, and salads. Yummy.

2 heads green cabbage

1 large beet, shredded

2 tart green apples,
  cored and shredded

2 cups chopped dinosaur kale
  or broccoli

1 (2-inch) piece fresh ginger,
  peeled and minced

1 (2-inch) piece fresh turmeric root,
  peeled and minced (optional)

6 cloves garlic, minced
  (omit for pitta)

Remove 3 large, whole leaves from the cabbage and set aside. Chop or shred the remaining cabbage and put it in a very large bowl. Add all the remaining ingredients. Mix well.

Transfer the cabbage mixture to a two-gallon, wide-mouthed, glass or ceramic crock or jar. (Do not use aluminum or other metals; they will inhibit the fermentation process.) Gently pack down the vegetables so that the crock or jar is about two-thirds full and the vegetables are firmly and evenly compressed.

Place the 3 reserved cabbage leaves over the vegetables. Put a large plate or bowl over the cabbage leaves, covering as much of the leaves as possible. Weigh down the plate or bowl. (A jug of water, a bottle of wine, or another heavy object will work.) Cover loosely with a dish towel. Store in a dark place for 7 to 10 days at room temperature. (If room temperature is above 75 degrees, fermentation may occur in 5 to 7 days.) The longer the fermentation, the stronger the flavor and potency.

Remove the weights and plate or bowl. Remove and discard the cabbage leaves and any discolored or moldy vegetables from the top layer. (The sauerkraut is safe to eat even if the top layer is moldy.) Stored in glass jars with plastic lids in the refrigerator, Raw Sauerkraut will keep for 6 months.

1 tablespoon brown
   mustard seeds

Juice of 1 orange

Juice of 1 lime

Juice of 1 lemon

2 tablespoons salt

Variation: You may substitute almost any vegetables as long as you keep the base of raw cabbage and salt. Some good substitutions include bok choy, celery, leek, fennel, collard greens, cauliflower, kohlrabi, and rutabaga.

Ruby Rye Kraut
(balances vata and kapha, increases pitta): Substitute red cabbage for green cabbage. Omit the apples and juices, and add 2 to 3 tablespoons of caraway seeds.

Extra-Special Sauce

Preparation Time: 10 minutes
Yield: 1 cup

My first paying job as an ayurvedic practitioner was to translate the basic makings of a McDonald's Big Mac into a healthful, ayurvedic sandwich. It was quite the remarkable task and a fun place to start my training as a chef. Try this Extra-Special Sauce in the Big Tempeh Mac (page 105) or as a yummy sandwich spread.

½ **cup Vegan Mayonnaise (page 75) or prepared vegan mayonnaise**

2 **tablespoons Faux French Dressing (page 61)**

½ **teaspoon ground coriander**

½ **teaspoon dill weed**

1 **tablespoon raw agave nectar or maple syrup**

1 **teaspoon cider vinegar**

⅛ **teaspoon salt**

1 **tablespoon minced green onions or leeks (omit for pitta)**

1 **teaspoon Fresh Mango Ketchup (page 80) or prepared ketchup (optional)**

2 **tablespoons Raw Sauerkraut (page 82) or prepared raw sauerkraut (optional)**

Whisk the Vegan Mayonnaise, Faux French Dressing, coriander, dill, agave nectar, vinegar, and salt until smooth. Stir in the green onions and the optional Fresh Mango Ketchup and Raw Sauerkraut. Stored in a covered container in the refrigerator, Extra-Special Sauce will keep for 2 weeks.

Avocado-Lime Dressing

decreases vata and pitta
increases kapha

Preparation Time: 15 minutes
Yield: 4 servings

Avocado is excellent brain food. Its monounsaturated fat helps lower cholesterol, and its antioxidants and vitamin E contribute to cell regeneration and beautiful skin. In essence, this recipe will make you beautiful and smart. Plus, it tastes really, really good.

---

1 large avocado

Juice of 1 lime

2 tablespoons olive oil

1 teaspoon salt

1 tablespoon dried dill weed

Put all the ingredients in a blender or food processor. Process until smooth and creamy, stopping occasionally to scrape down the blender jar or work bowl. If the dressing is too thick, add another tablespoon of olive oil and process again. Stored in a covered container in the refrigerator, Avocado-Lime Dressing will keep for 3 days.

Ginger, Daikon, and Beet Garnish

decreases vata and kapha
increases pitta

Preparation Time: 10 minutes
Yield: About 1 cup

This garnish enlivens soups and stews, especially for vata and kapha. It's aesthetically beautiful, as well as warming and cleansing for the blood and liver.

---

1 (2-inch) piece fresh ginger, peeled and grated

½ small daikon radish, grated

1 small red beet, peeled and grated

Juice of ½ lemon

2 tablespoons chopped fresh cilantro (optional)

Combine all the ingredients in a small bowl. Stored in a covered container in the refrigerator, Ginger, Daikon, and Beet Garnish will keep for 1 week.

Note: Beets and ginger help build blood cells. Cilantro adds a beautiful color and taste, and is used in ayurveda as a blood cleanser.

Gado Gado Sauce

decreases vata and kapha
increases pitta slightly

Preparation Time: 10 minutes
Yield: About 2 cups

Spicy, sweet, and satisfying, this is my answer for a hearty peanut sauce. It tastes delicious with Steamed Collard Wraps (page 108).

---

1 cup water

2 tablespoons grated fresh ginger

2 tablespoons raw agave nectar
   or maple syrup

1 teaspoon green curry paste
   (omit for pitta)

1 cup raw almond butter

1 teaspoon ground cumin

1 teaspoon ground coriander

1 teaspoon ground cinnamon

1 teaspoon salt

½ teaspoon ground pepper

Bring the water and ginger to a boil in a covered, medium saucepan. Remove from the heat. Remove the cover. Let cool.

Combine all the remaining ingredients in a medium bowl. Stir in the ginger and ginger cooking water until well blended.

Fresh Cucumber Raita

Preparation Time: 10 minutes
Yield: About 2½ cups

Raita is a traditional Indian condiment, most often served alongside Indian breads, curries, and dals, or as a dip for fresh vegetables. This raita is quick, easy, cool, and sweet, making it a great condiment for pitta.

1 small cucumber, seeded and coarsely grated

2 cups plain coconut yogurt or Creamy Coconut Kefir (page 44)

¼ cup chopped fresh cilantro

1 teaspoon cumin seeds

1 teaspoon ground cumin

1 teaspoon ground coriander

1 teaspoon salt

½ teaspoon ground turmeric

½ teaspoon ground ginger (omit for pitta)

½ teaspoon ground pepper (omit for pitta)

¼ teaspoon chili powder (omit for pitta)

⅛ teaspoon ground cinnamon or nutmeg

Combine all the ingredients in a large bowl. Mix well. Refrigerate for at least 1 hour before serving.

Note: For a thicker raita, stir in 1 tablespoon of lecithin powder until well blended.

Yummus

Preparation Time: 15 minutes, plus 4 to 6 hours soaking time
Yield: About 4 cups

In all my years of experimenting with chickpea dishes, this is my pièce de résistance. It's a delightful party dip that goes well with slices of sweet apples, juicy jicama, and red radishes, and sticks of raw zucchini or celery.

---

1 cup raw pumpkin seeds

2 cups water

2 (15-ounce) cans or 3½ cups
  cooked chickpeas, drained
  and rinsed

1 cup young coconut juice

½ cup freshly squeezed lemon juice

3 cloves garlic

1 (1-inch) piece fresh ginger,
  peeled and minced

½ bunch cilantro

1 avocado

1 tablespoon raw tahini

½ cup olive oil

1 tablespoon raw agave nectar
  or maple syrup

2 teaspoons salt

Soak the pumpkin seeds in a small bowl with the water for 4 to 6 hours. Drain and transfer to a food processor or blender. Add all the remaining ingredients. Process for 30 seconds or until smooth, stopping occasionally to scrape down the work bowl or blender jar. If the Yummus is too thick or pasty, add a few more tablespoons of coconut juice and process again.

Butternut Squash–Crusted Pizza,
page 94

Tempeh Reuben, page 105,
with Ayurvedic Home Fries, page 42

Cashew-Cheddar Cheese

balances vata
increases pitta and kapha slightly

Preparation Time: 10 minutes
Yield: 1½ cups; 2 to 4 servings

This tastes amazingly like a velvety, herb-infused cheese. It has even fooled people who couldn't wait to get their hands on some meat and dairy cheese—not that I meant to fool them, of course.

½ red bell pepper,
  seeded and chopped

¼ cup water

1 cup raw cashews

1 tablespoon raw tahini

2 tablespoons nutritional
  yeast flakes

1½ teaspoons salt

1 teaspoon ground cumin

2 teaspoons onion powder

2 to 4 cloves garlic, minced
  (omit for pitta)

Juice of 1 lemon

⅛ teaspoon cayenne
  or ground pepper
  (omit for pitta)

Put all the ingredients in a food processor or a blender. Process until smooth, stopping occasionally to scrape down the work bowl or blender jar. Serve as a dip or spread.

Note: If you are sensitive to red bell peppers or vegetables of the nightshade family, substitute ½ small jicama for the red bell pepper and add 1 pinch ground cinnamon.

Italian Cashew-Cheddar Cheese
(balances vata and kapha, increases pitta slightly): Substitute 1 teaspoon of dried marjoram, 1 teaspoon of dried basil, and 1 teaspoon of dried oregano for the cumin. Use 1 teaspoon of the onion powder and 4 cloves of garlic.

Palmesan Cheese

decreases vata
increases pitta and kapha slightly

Preparation Time: 5 minutes
Yield: About 1½ cups

A nutritional powerhouse, Palmesan Cheese complements the Vegan Caesar Salad (page 69) and any meal where a little flavor and pizzazz is in order.

---

2 tablespoons almonds or pine nuts

2 tablespoons nutritional yeast flakes

2 tablespoons raw sesame seeds

¼ teaspoon salt

¼ teaspoon onion powder

¼ teaspoon lemon zest (optional)

Put all the ingredients in a food processor. Process for about 10 seconds, or until the almonds are finely ground, stopping occasionally to scrape down the work bowl. Stored in a covered container in the refrigerator, Palmesan Cheese will keep for 6 weeks.

Raw-Onion Side

increases vata and pitta
decreases kapha

Preparation Time: 5 minutes
Yield: About 1 cup

This side dish can accompany almost any savory meal, especially for kapha, who will greatly benefit from its pungent warmth.

---

1 large red onion, minced

Juice of 1 lemon

1 teaspoon fennel seeds

½ teaspoon salt

½ teaspoon ground black pepper

Combine all the ingredients in a small bowl.

Dad's Cranberry Sauce

increases vata and pitta
decreases kapha

Preparation Time: About 30 minutes
Yield: About 3 cups

SEE PHOTO FACING PAGE 121.

I always loved the food my dad made, and this sauce is no exception. Pitta should substitute apple or pear juice for the orange juice as the orange juice may seem too acidic. But the time of year when this is likely to be made, in late fall and winter, is a good time to raise a little internal heat.

1½ pounds fresh
  or frozen cranberries

¾ cup dehydrated cane juice,
  date sugar, or maple syrup,
  plus more to taste

1½ cups orange juice, apple juice,
  or pear juice

1 tablespoon ground cardamom

1 tablespoon ground cinnamon

Bring the cranberries, dehydrated cane juice, and orange juice to a boil in a large saucepan over medium-high heat. Immediately decrease the heat to medium. Cook, stirring constantly, until the sauce is the consistency of chunky jam. Stir in the cardamom, cinnamon, and additional dehydrated cane juice to taste. If the sauce seems too thick, stir in ¼ cup of water.

Variation: Add 1 cup of fresh or frozen blueberries, chopped persimmons, raspberries, chopped pears, or a chopped, steamed beet with the cranberries.

CHAPTER 10

Main Meal Dishes

ALL SENSE OF CONTROL IS LOST when we're at a great party or restaurant and the meal is just too fabulous to pass up. Many of us rely on eating outside the home, where we're not in control of the ingredients in our food. The downside to all this is that we often consume greasy cooked oils, sticky flours, white sugar, and salt-laden fare, which can leave us feeling full, bloated, heavy, and cranky.

If going out to eat is a staple of your lifestyle, there's no need to force yourself to eat at home. It's completely possible to incorporate ayurvedic nutrition into almost any meal, even to a small degree. Here's a quick guide to integrating healthful practices when you go out to eat, followed by recipes for delicious main dishes for cooking at home.

Tips on Eating Out for Vata

Dip yeasty breads into olive oil sprinkled with cracked black pepper. Restaurants will almost always provide you with a side of both. Choose well-spiced curries at Indian and Thai restaurants, and cooked grains, soups, and broths with lots of vegetables, ginger, and rice noodles at any Asian restaurant. Sip mint or ginger tea throughout your meal, and avoid all iced drinks (including iced water).

Tips on Eating Out for Pitta

Stick with Japanese restaurants, salad bars, and raw food restaurants, where an abundance of light, fresh vegetables are served. Avoid fried foods. Choose soups (except for tomato), spring rolls, coleslaws, steamed grains, and bean dishes, with fresh fruit as dessert.

Tips on Eating Out for Kapha

Sip hot or room temperature water with lemon, and order vegetable soups, light curries, and fresh salads. Avoid bread at all costs. Order brown rice instead of white rice when you can, and ask for it to be sprinkled with cracked black pepper. Choose raw, steamed, grilled, and baked foods, and fresh fruit or dark chocolate as dessert. Avoid sweet-and-sour soups and all fried, heavy foods.

Butternut Squash-Crusted Pizza

balances vata, pitta, and kapha

Preparation Time: 1 hour, 15 minutes
Yield: 6 to 8 servings

SEE PHOTO FACING PAGE 88.

I love pizza, and this protein-rich crust rocks the house. It's gluten-free, savory, and so easy to make. Be creative, and enjoy it with any variety of toppings you'd like.

Crust

1 large butternut squash, peeled, seeded, and cut into large chunks

1 tablespoon egg replacer

4 tablespoons water

2 tablespoons melted coconut oil

1 cup cornmeal

¾ cup amaranth flour or quinoa flour

½ cup coconut flour

2 teaspoons salt

2 teaspoons baking powder

2 teaspoons ground cumin

1 tablespoon herbes de Provence or Italian herb seasoning mix

Preheat the oven to 350 degrees F. Lightly oil a pizza pan with coconut oil.

To make the crust, place a steamer basket in a large saucepan with about 1 cup of water. Bring the water to a boil. Put the squash in the steamer basket. Cover. Steam for about 20 minutes, or until the squash is fork-tender. Drain. Transfer the squash to a blender or food processor.

Whisk the egg replacer with the water in a small bowl until smooth. Pour it into the blender or food processor with the squash. Add the coconut oil. Process until smooth, stopping occasionally to scrape down the blender jar or work bowl. Set aside.

Mix the cornmeal, amaranth flour, coconut flour, salt, and baking powder in a large bowl. Stir in the cumin and herbes de Provence. Pour the squash mixture into the cornmeal mixture. Stir until combined. Pour the batter into the prepared pan. Bake for 15 minutes.

Topping

1 tablespoon coconut oil

1 red onion, chopped

1 teaspoon salt

1 teaspoon fennel seeds

1 medium sweet potato or yam,
   peeled and julienned

¼ bunch dinosaur kale, chopped

2 cloves garlic, minced

½ cup chopped sun-dried tomatoes

¼ cup basil leaves

¼ cup Garlic Dream Sauce
   (page 81), or ¼ cup shredded
   vegan Monterey jack cheese

1 avocado, sliced, for garnish

¼ cup pitted olives or raw olives,
   for garnish

To make the topping, melt the coconut oil in a large, shallow skillet over medium-high heat. Add the onion, salt, and fennel seeds. Cook about 3 minutes, or until the onion is soft. Add the sweet potato and cook for 5 minutes, or until fork-tender. Add the kale and garlic and cook for another 2 minutes.

Spread the sweet potato mixture over the crust. Place the sun-dried tomatoes and basil on the top. Drizzle with the Garlic Dream Sauce. Bake for 10 minutes. Garnish with the avocado and olives if desired.

Vegetable-Root Bake

decreases vata, pitta, and kapha

Preparation Time: 45 minutes
Yield: 4 to 6 servings

Simple, versatile, and flavorful, even the leftovers taste great. It's a nice alternative to roasting vegetables in oil.

½ cup water

4 large Jerusalem artichokes
  (sunchokes) or red potatoes,
  cut into ¼-inch-thick slices

1 large sweet potato, cut into
  ½-inch cubes

1 parsnip, cut into
  ¼-inch-thick slices

1 bulb fennel, or carrot, sliced thin

1 small leek, cut in half lengthwise,
  then cut into 1-inch pieces

1 (2-inch) piece fresh ginger, peeled
  and minced

¼ cup toasted sea palm (optional)

1 teaspoon salt, plus more to taste

1 teaspoon fennel seeds

1 teaspoon cumin seeds

1 teaspoon dried rosemary or
  3 tablespoons fresh rosemary leaves

Salt

Freshly ground pepper

¼ cup flaxseed oil, hempseed oil,
  or olive oil, for garnish

Preheat the oven to 400 degrees F. Pour the water into a large, rimmed baking sheet or 14 x 11-inch glass baking pan. Combine the artichokes, sweet potato, parsnip, fennel, leek, ginger, optional sea palm, salt, fennel seeds, cumin, and rosemary in a large bowl. Transfer the vegetable mixture to the baking sheet. Bake for 25 minutes.

Stir the vegetables. Bake for another 15 to 20 minutes, or until they are lightly browned and fork-tender. Season with the salt and pepper. Drizzle each serving with 1 to 2 tablespoons of the oil.

Macrobiotic Brown Rice

Preparation Time: 45 minutes, plus 1 hour soak time
Yield: 2 to 4 servings

Taught to me by a macrobiotic-loving sweetheart of mine, this healing dish has saved me many times and in more ways than one. If a food could say, "I am here for you," this one would. Pair Macrobiotic Brown Rice with Miso Soup (page 121) or Fresh Ginger Tea (page 35) for a nourishing meal.

Rice

2 cups short-grain brown rice

8 cups water

½ teaspoon salt

Condiments

**4 sheets nori, torn into
    ¼-inch squares**

1 tablespoon olive oil

1 tablespoon Gomasio (page 77)

**1 teaspoon Bragg Liquid Aminos
    or coconut aminos**

To make the rice, soak it in 4 cups of the water in a medium bowl for at least 1 hour, or as long as 8 to 12 hours. Drain. Rinse the rice under running water, kneading it with your hands, for 1 minute. Drain again.

Transfer the rice to a medium saucepan with the salt and 4 cups of fresh water. Cover. Bring to a boil over medium-high heat. Decrease the heat to low. Simmer about 35 minutes, or until all of the water has been absorbed and the rice is tender. During the last 5 to 10 minutes of cooking, wipe away any condensation that may form on the underside of the lid with a dish towel. To serve, garnish each serving of rice with the condiments.

Spaghetti Squash

Preparation Time: 1 hour
Yield: 2 to 4 servings

Sattvic and grounding, squash is nourishing, balancing, and good for the spleen. Spaghetti Squash is a great-tasting main dish when topped with Amazing Pesto Chutney (page 74), Magical Mato Sauce (page 111), or Garlic Dream Sauce (page 81).

---

1 large spaghetti squash

½ cup water, plus more as needed

Preheat the oven to 375 degrees F. Pour the water into a 13 x 9-inch glass baking pan. Cut the ends off the squash and discard. Cut the squash in half lengthwise. Remove the seeds. Place each half cut-side down in the prepared pan. Bake for 45 minutes, or until the squash is fork-tender, adding another ½ cup water if necessary to prevent the squash from burning. Let cool for 5 to 10 minutes. The flesh will break into spaghetti-like strands as you scrape it out with a fork.

Note: This is also an easy way to bake other squash, such as butternut and acorn.

Crispy Mustard Vegetables

Preparation Time: 1 hour
Yield: 4 to 6 servings

Reminiscent of onion rings and french fries, Crispy Mustard Vegetables is much more healthful. I choose this recipe when I want to impress.

---

2 tablespoons stone-ground mustard

4 cloves garlic, minced

4 tablespoons olive oil

2 cups multigrain cereal flakes

1 teaspoon salt

1 tablespoon fennel seeds

1 teaspoon ground cumin

1 teaspoon dried dill weed

1 teaspoon dried rosemary

½ teaspoon ground coriander

1 small bulb fennel, thinly sliced

1 large sweet potato, cut in half lengthwise and sliced into ¼-inch half-circles

1 large red potato, cut in half lengthwise and sliced into ¼-inch half-circles

1 leek, sliced lengthwise then cut into 1½-inch pieces

1 small red onion, thinly sliced (omit for pitta)

Preheat the oven to 375 degrees F. In a medium bowl, mix the mustard, garlic, and oil. Set aside.

Put the cereal in a food processor or blender. Process to a coarse meal. Transfer the meal to a medium bowl. Add the salt, fennel seeds, cumin, dill, rosemary, and coriander. Mix well. Set aside.

Add the fennel bulb, sweet potato, red potato, leek, and onion to the mustard mixture. Stir until well coated. Pour the vegetables into the cereal mixture. Stir to coat the vegetables. Spread the vegetables in a single layer on a large, rimmed baking sheet. Bake about 45 minutes, or until the vegetables are golden brown.

Rejuvenation Stew

decreases vata
balances pitta and kapha

Preparation Time: 40 minutes
Yield: 3 to 4 servings

This is my favorite soup to eat in the fall when vata (plus everyone else) needs grounding and nourishment. Incorporate as many vegetables into this stew as you'd like, and serve with a tasty slice of toasted sprouted-grain bread.

---

1 cup unsweetened Almond Milk (page 34) or prepared almond milk

1 cup coconut milk

2 cups water

1 (2-inch) piece fresh ginger, peeled and minced

1 large sweet potato or 2 red potatoes, scrubbed and cut into ½-inch chunks

1 bulb fennel, julienned

1 small leek or red onion, minced

1 teaspoon salt

1 teaspoon fennel seeds

1 teaspoon ground turmeric

½ cup raw, wild nori or sea palm, chopped or crumbled

½ bunch collard greens, minced

¼ cup goji berries

1 tablespoon miso

¼ teaspoon ground pepper (optional)

Heat the Almond Milk, coconut milk, and water in a large soup pot over medium-high heat. Add the ginger. Cook for about 5 minutes. Decrease the heat to medium. Add the sweet potato, fennel bulb, leek, salt, fennel seeds, and turmeric. Cook for 10 minutes, or until the fennel bulb is fork-tender.

Stir in the nori, collard greens, and goji berries. Remove from the heat. Stir in the miso until most of it has dissolved. Cover. Let stand for 5 minutes. Remove the nori before serving and season with pepper if desired.

Variation: For a potent immune-boosting soup, add 1 ounce (or about 2 sticks) of astragalus with the ginger.

Winter Vegetable Stew

Preparation Time: 45 minutes
Yield: About 4 servings

This is a great dish to make with someone you love, especially in winter when spending time together in the kitchen feels so nurturing.

4 cups water

1 small acorn, kabocha, or butternut squash, peeled and cut into 1-inch cubes

¼ cup raw, wild nori

1 teaspoon green curry paste (omit for pitta)

1 teaspoon salt

1 (2-inch) piece fresh ginger, peeled and sliced

1 leek, cut lengthwise, then sliced into half moons

1 cup Brussels sprouts or snow peas

1 teaspoon miso

1 red onion, minced

1 cup chopped broccoli florets

½ bunch dill weed or tarragon, minced

½ teaspoon ground pepper (omit for pitta)

Heat the water in a large saucepan over medium-high heat. Add the squash, nori, curry paste, salt, and ginger. Cover. Bring to a boil. Decrease the heat to medium. Cook for 5 minutes.

Add the leek and Brussels sprouts. Cook for another 7 minutes. Add the miso, onion, and broccoli. Cover. Decrease the heat to medium-low. Cook for another 3 to 5 minutes, or until the broccoli is bright green and still slightly firm.

Remove from the heat. Stir in the dill. Season with the pepper.

Zucchini Pasta

decreases vata and pitta
balances kapha

Preparation Time: 10 minutes
Yield: 2 to 3 servings

This dish is a surprisingly simple and awesome alternative to pasta. Top it with your favorite pasta sauce, or try Magical 'Mato Sauce (page 111), or a mix of olive oil, garlic, salt, and slivered almonds.

---

1 cup water

2 zucchini

Place a steamer basket in a large pot with the water. Bring the water to a boil.

Meanwhile, use a vegetable peeler to cut long ribbons of zucchini by drawing the peeler down all sides of the zucchini until you have peeled the entire squash into "noodles." Put them in the steamer. Steam for 3 to 4 minutes, or until the zucchini is crisp-tender.

Note: Pitta may want to skip the steaming of the zucchini and enjoy this pasta raw.

Whole-Grain Nori Rolls

decreases vata and kapha
balances pitta

Preparation Time: 45 minutes
Yield: 4 servings

Nori is a type of seaweed packed with protein, minerals, and vitamins. When combined with a hearty grain, such as quinoa, brown rice, or amaranth, it yields an energizing, good-to-go, high-protein meal that kids and adults tend to love.

1½ tablespoons cider vinegar
 or coconut vinegar

1 teaspoon freshly grated lime zest

Juice of 1 lime

1½ tablespoons raw agave nectar
 or maple syrup

3 tablespoons olive oil

1 teaspoon salt

2 cups room temperature, cooked
 quinoa, brown rice, or amaranth

1 large cucumber,
 seeded and julienned

1 large carrot or beet, julienned

1 large avocado, julienned

2 to 4 cloves garlic, minced
 (omit for pitta)

1 (1-inch) piece fresh ginger,
 peeled and minced

½ cup ground Brazil nuts,
 raw cashews, or pine nuts

½ cup fresh basil leaves

½ cup sunflower sprouts

4 sheets nori

Whisk the vinegar, lime zest, lime juice, agave nectar, oil, and salt in a small bowl. Add the quinoa and mix well. Set aside.

Prepare the cucumber, carrot, avocado, garlic, ginger, nuts, basil, and sprouts and place them within easy reach.

Place 1 nori sheet shiny-side down on your workspace. Press ½ cup of the quinoa mixture onto the lower third of the nori sheet. Place the cucumber, carrot, and avocado strips, garlic, ginger, nuts, basil, and sprouts on top of the quinoa mixture so that they cover the width of the nori.

Carefully fold the side of the nori closest to you over the filling and roll it up into a snug roll. Place the rolled nori on a plate. Repeat with the remaining ingredients. Serve as is, cut the nori rolls in half diagonally, or cut them into bite-sized, sushi pieces.

Creamy Miso Lentils

Preparation Time: 30 minutes
Yield: About 4 cups; 4 servings

These lentils are so smooth and creamy, they taste like a healthful version of refried beans.

---

2 cups red or yellow lentils or
   split green peas

4 cups water

3 tablespoons miso (any variety)

1 teaspoon fennel seeds

¾ teaspoon salt

1 teaspoon ground nutmeg

½ teaspoon ground cumin

Two (2- to 3-inch) pieces raw,
   wild nori

½ cup hot water

Bring the lentils and the 4 cups of water to a boil in a large soup pot over medium-high heat. Stir in the miso, fennel seeds, salt, nutmeg, cumin, and nori. Cover. Decrease the heat to low. Simmer for about 20 minutes, stirring often, to prevent the lentils from sticking to the pan. Stir in the ½ cup of hot water. Simmer until the lentils are smooth and creamy.

Tempeh Reuben

Preparation Time: 40 minutes
Yield: 2 servings

SEE PHOTO FACING PAGE 89.

Kids and grown-ups alike love this dish every time I serve it. Plate it with a side of Ayurvedic Home Fries (page 42), Faux French Dressing (61), and a salad. It's dynamite.

1 large portobello mushroom, cut into long, thin slices

2 tablespoons sesame oil

2 tablespoons tamari, Bragg Liquid Aminos, or coconut aminos

4 slices sprouted-grain rye bread or raw sunflower seed bread

2 teaspoons olive oil

2 teaspoons stone-ground mustard

¼ cup Raw Sauerkraut (page 82) or prepared raw sauerkraut

½ teaspoon ground pepper

½ teaspoon ground coriander

½ cup sunflower sprouts

1 serving (4 slices) Baked Tempeh (page 126)

1 tomato, sliced thin (optional)

Preheat the oven to 350 degrees F. Put the mushroom, sesame oil, and tamari in a wide, shallow bowl. Toss to coat the mushroom. Set aside.

Toast the bread in a toaster. Place the 2 slices of toast on a plate. Drizzle each slice with 1 teaspoon of the olive oil. Spread each slice with 1 teaspoon of the mustard. Put 2 tablespoons of the Raw Sauerkraut on each slice. Sprinkle with the pepper and coriander. Top each with ¼ cup of the sprouts.

Place 2 slices of the Baked Tempeh on each slice of bread. Top with the marinated mushrooms. Serve open-faced with the optional tomato slices on the side.

Big Tempeh Mac
(balances vata and pitta, increases kapha): Substitute seeded and sprouted bread for the rye and 2 tablespoons Extra-Special Sauce (page 84) for the olive oil. Use 2 thin slices of red onion, 2 leaves of romaine lettuce, and 2 teaspoons of Fresh Mango Ketchup (page 80).

Mung Bean Stew

Preparation Time: 1 hour, plus soaking time
Yield: 6 cups; 4 to 6 servings

Allow me to introduce you to the queen of legumes, the mung bean. It's versatile, digestible by every dosha, and filled with essential amino acids.

1 cup whole mung beans

1½ teaspoons coconut oil

1 teaspoon fennel seeds

1 teaspoon cumin seeds

1 (1-inch) piece fresh ginger, peeled and minced

½ small leek or 2 green onions, minced (optional)

1 stalk celery, minced

1 heaping cup ¼-inch thick carrot slices

4 cups water

2 tablespoons freshly squeezed lemon juice

1½ teaspoons salt

1 sweet potato, scrubbed and diced

1 red or purple potato, scrubbed and diced

½ bunch kale, shredded (about 2 cups)

2 teaspoons curry powder

Soak the mung beans overnight (8 to 12 hours) in a medium bowl in enough water to cover. Drain and rinse.

Melt the coconut oil in a large saucepan over medium-high heat. Add the fennel, cumin, and ginger. Cook and stir for 1 minute. Add the leek, celery, and carrots. Cook and stir for another 1 or 2 minutes. Add the mung beans, water, lemon juice, and salt. Cover. Cook for 30 minutes over medium heat, stirring occasionally.

Add the sweet potato and red potato. Cook for another 15 minutes, or until the sweet potato is fork-tender. Remove from the heat. Stir in the kale. Cover. Set aside for 5 minutes. Stir in the curry powder before serving.

Variation: Top this stew in the spring with colorful Ginger, Daikon, and Beet Garnish (page 85) and in the winter with Fried Soup Onions (page 129).

Mom's Mac and Cheese

Preparation time: 1 hour and 15 minutes
Yield: 8 to 10 servings

Since I was a kid, whenever I've felt down in the dumps or needed extra love, my mom has offered to make me her macaroni and cheese. It's been a favorite my whole life, and it really makes me appreciate my mom. Here's my vegan, ayurvedic version of her nourishing classic.

8 cups water

4 cups rice, quinoa or whole wheat elbow macaroni

3 tablespoons plus 2 teaspoons coconut oil

3 cups unsweetened Almond Milk (page 34) or prepared almond milk

2 tablespoons stone-ground mustard

1 teaspoon salt

1 teaspoon ground coriander

1 teaspoon ground turmeric

2 teaspoons cumin seeds

1 tablespoon dried rosemary

2 teaspoons dried basil

1 cup Garlic Dream Sauce (page 81) or shredded vegan Cheddar cheese

¼ cup chopped fresh basil or parsley, plus more for garnish

Bring the water to a boil in a large, deep pot. Add the macaroni and 1 teaspoon of the coconut oil. Cook for about 7 minutes, or until the macaroni is al dente, stirring once or twice to prevent the pasta from sticking to the pot. Drain and rinse. Return the macaroni to the pot.

Preheat the oven to 375 degrees F. Lightly oil a 13 x 9-inch glass baking pan with 1 teaspoon of the coconut oil.

Heat the Almond Milk in a medium saucepan over medium-high heat for 1 minute. Add the mustard, 3 tablespoons of the coconut oil, salt, coriander, turmeric, cumin, rosemary, and basil. Stir until the coconut oil is melted. Remove from the heat. Stir in the Garlic Dream Sauce. Pour the sauce over the macaroni. Stir until well combined.

Pour the macaroni mixture into the prepared pan. Bake for 35 minutes. Increase the heat to 425 degrees F and bake for another 10 minutes, or until the top is browned. Garnish with the basil if desired.

Steamed Collard Wraps

increases vata
decreases pitta and kapha

Preparation Time: 35 minutes
Yield: 6 to 8 servings

SEE PHOTO FACING PAGE 120.

These make a beautiful dish for a potluck or dinner party. They make great appetizers, too. Serve them as is or paired with Gado Gado Sauce (page 86).

---

2 sweet potatoes, julienned

1 bunch collard greens

1 red bell pepper or jicama, julienned

2 avocados, julienned

1 beet, shredded

1 carrot, shredded

½ cup chopped raw macadamia or pine nuts

½ cup sunflower sprouts (optional)

1 (1-inch) piece fresh ginger, peeled and minced

4 cloves garlic, minced (omit for pitta)

1 (1-inch) piece fresh turmeric root, peeled and minced (optional)

½ cup Creamy Cucumber-Tahini Dressing (page 72)

Place a steamer basket in a medium saucepan with about ½ cup water. Bring the water to a boil. Put the sweet potatoes in the steamer basket. Cover. Steam for 5 minutes, or until fork-tender. Transfer the potatoes to a bowl or colander. Set aside.

Meanwhile, remove the stems from each collard leaf by carefully slicing along each side of the stem so that the leaves are cut in half, and each half remains intact. Set aside. Reserve the stems for another use. (See Note.)

Put the steamer basket back into the saucepan and add the collard leaves. Steam for 30 seconds, or just until softened. Transfer the collard greens to a separate bowl or colander.

Prepare the remaining ingredients and place them within easy reach.

Place 2 collard leaf halves lengthwise on top of each other. Place 1 or 2 strips each of the sweet potatoes, bell pepper, and avocados across the lower third of the collard leaves. Top with 1 tablespoon each of the beet, carrot, macadamia nuts, and optional sunflower sprouts. Sprinkle with 1 teaspoon each of the ginger, garlic, and optional turmeric. Drizzle with 2 tablespoons of the Creamy Cucumber-Tahini Dressing.

Carefully fold the end of the collard leaves over the filling and roll up into a snug wrap. Place the wrap on a plate. Repeat with the remaining collard leaves and ingredients.

Note: Use the collard stems in Perfect Spring Soup (page 119) or Brew Broth Stock (page 114).

Palak Paneer

Preparation Time: 1 hour
Yield: 4 to 6 servings

Here is a health-giving, ayurvedic version of my favorite traditional Indian dish, spinach with vegan farmer's cheese. Serve this with brown rice and Vegan Mango Lassi (page 40).

1 tablespoon coconut oil

1 teaspoon brown mustard seeds

1 large red onion, diced
  (omit for pitta)

1 (1-inch) piece fresh ginger,
  peeled and minced

2 tablespoons ground coriander

2 teaspoons ground cumin

1 teaspoon chili powder (optional)

2 bunches spinach, collard greens,
  or dinosaur kale, chopped

2 teaspoons minced garlic

2 teaspoons salt

2 teaspoons garam masala
  or curry powder

¼ cup raw cashews

1 cup Vegan Paneer Cheese
  (page 134)

Melt the coconut oil with the mustard seeds in a medium to large skillet over medium-high heat. When the mustard seeds pop, add the onion, ginger, coriander, cumin, and optional chili powder. Cook and stir for 1 minute. Add the spinach, garlic, salt, and garam masala. Cook and stir for another 3 to 4 minutes, or until the spinach is wilted.

Remove from the heat. Immediately stir in the raw cashews and Vegan Paneer Cheese.

Magical 'Mato Lasagne

decreases vata
balances pitta
increases kapha slightly

Preparation Time: 2 hours
Yield: 8 to 10 servings

The tomato-less sauce is sweet and savory in all the right ways. The lasagne's heartiness may weigh down kapha, so pair this dish with a salad to make the meal lighter.

2½ tablespoons coconut oil

10 ounces brown rice or whole wheat lasagna noodles

2 teaspoons olive oil

1 tablespoon cumin seeds

1 teaspoon salt

1 leek, minced

4 cloves garlic, minced

2 tablespoons peeled, minced fresh ginger

2 small zucchini, cut in half lengthwise and sliced into ¼-inch half-moons

1 bunch dinosaur kale, cut in half lengthwise and coarsely chopped

2 bunches spinach, stems removed

1⅓ tablespoons Italian herb seasoning mix or herbes de Provence

3 slices gluten-free brown rice bread or sprouted grain bread

2 tablespoons chopped, fresh basil leaves

1 teaspoon salt

4 cups Magical 'Mato Sauce (opposite page)

2 cups Garlic Dream Sauce (page 81) (optional)

Preheat the oven to 350 degrees F. Lightly oil a 13 x 9-inch glass baking pan with 1 or 2 teaspoons of the coconut oil.

Cook the noodles according to the package directions with the olive oil. Drain. Set aside.

Melt 1 tablespoon of the coconut oil in a large skillet over medium heat. Cook and stir the cumin, salt, leek, garlic, and ginger for 1 minute. Add the zucchini and cook and stir for another 3 minutes. Add the kale, spinach, and 1 tablespoon of the Italian seasoning. Cook and stir about 3 minutes, or until the kale and spinach start to wilt. Remove from the heat. Set aside.

Toast the bread in a toaster until crispy and golden brown. Break the toast into pieces. Put them in a food processor with the basil, the remaining coconut oil, and salt. Process until it forms coarse crumbs.

Pour 1 cup of the Magical 'Mato Sauce into the prepared pan. Place the noodles in a layer over the sauce. Pour another cup of the Magical 'Mato Sauce or 1 cup of the optional Garlic Dream Sauce over the noodles. Top with half of the kale mixture. Repeat. Sprinkle with the bread crumbs. Bake for 30 minutes. Let cool for 5 minutes before serving.

Magical 'Mato Sauce

Preparation Time: 45 minutes
Yield: 6 cups

8 cups water

1 butternut squash, peeled
   and cut into 2-inch chunks

4 carrots, cut into 2-inch chunks

1 large beet, cut into 2-inch chunks

3 bay leaves

2 teaspoons coconut oil

½ bunch kale, including stems,
   shredded

4 cloves garlic, minced
   (omit for pitta)

1 teaspoon dried oregano

1 teaspoon dried basil

1 teaspoon dried thyme

2 teaspoons fresh rosemary,
   or 1 teaspoon dried

1 teaspoon salt

Juice of 1 lime

Bring the water to a boil in a large saucepan over medium-high heat. Add the squash, carrots, beet, and bay leaves. Boil for 15 minutes, or until the squash is fork-tender. Drain, reserving at least 2 cups of the cooking water. Remove and discard the bay leaves. Let the vegetables cool for a few minutes.

Meanwhile, melt the coconut oil in a large saucepan over medium-high heat. Stir in the kale, garlic, oregano, basil, thyme, rosemary, and salt. Cook and stir for 3 minutes, or until the kale is soft and wilted. Remove from the heat.

Put half of the squash mixture, 1 cup of the reserved cooking water, and half of the kale mixture in a food processor or blender. Process until smooth, stopping occasionally to scrape down the work bowl or blender jar. Pour into a large saucepan. Repeat with the remaining squash mixture, 1 cup of the cooking water, and remaining kale mixture. Simmer the sauce over low heat for 5 to 10 minutes, stirring often. Mix in the lime juice just before removing from the heat.

Note: Magical 'Mato Sauce also makes a great addition to Zucchini Pasta (page 102). Because this recipe yields a large quantity of sauce, you may choose to serve it as a Magical 'Mato Soup, pairing it with Quinoa Pancakes (page 51).

Soups

Just thinking about soups and stews makes me want to get cozy. Their warmth and heartiness make them the mama of all other recipes in this book.

Incorporating fresh, seasonal vegetables that are best suited to your constitution is the right way to go. (See the lists of foods for your dosha in Chapter 4, beginning on page 19.) If ingredients listed in this section don't appeal to you, substitute vegetables that do. Similarly, replace hard-to-find or out-of-season vegetables with ones that are easily obtainable in your area and climate. These recipes are meant to be forgiving and open to experimentation with the flavors, textures, and vegetables you love.

The Formula for Making Soups

I like to use a food processor or a high-powered blender when making smooth, blended soups. If you prefer a chunkier consistency to your soups, skip the blending step. You can pour blended or chunky soups over cooked whole grains, such as pearled barley, quinoa, or brown rice, to add more texture and protein to a meal.

What You Need

Vegetables are the base for most soups. Use vegetables that have been steamed, baked, boiled, or roasted.

Spices and seasonings, such as cider vinegar or ume plum vinegar, green curry paste, ginger, garlic, maple syrup, miso, salt (see page 28), sea vegetables, and a whole world of spices and fresh herbs

Liquid bases, such as Almond Milk (page 34), Brew Broth Stock (page 114), coconut milk, Miso Soup (page 121), vegetable broth, and water

Proteins, such as almonds, beans, Brazil nuts, cashews, lentils, pine nuts, pumpkin seeds, sunflower seeds, and walnuts

Garnishes or toppings, such as Fried Soup Onions (page 129), Ginger, Daikon, and Beet Garnish (page 85), chopped fresh herbs, lecithin powder, Raw Sauerkraut (page 82), and coconut yogurt

The Basic Process

Boil, steam, bake, or roast vegetables in any combination you want. Be creative and daring, and trust yourself. A great practice is to choose, every so often, one new vegetable that you've never tried before. You'll often be delighted by what you discover. Vegetables are delicious and highly adaptable—so you're not likely to make a bad combination. Keep in mind that orange vegetables (like carrots and sweet potatoes) yield a brown soup when puréed with dark green vegetables (such as kale and collard greens), so these color combinations are usually best left chunky.

In a food processor or blender, put your customized blend of seasonings, protein, and cooked vegetables. Add a liquid, and process. Transfer the blended mixture to a large saucepan or soup pot. Cook it over low heat. Season to taste. Serve with a garnish, and voilà—it's soup.

Note: One rule of thumb is to balance vegetable combinations in terms of rasa, or taste. If you want to make a sweet soup to balance vata or pitta, use mostly sweet root vegetables, such as sweet potatoes and beets. If you're making a root vegetable-based soup for kapha, use some roots that are less sweet, such as burdock root, radishes, turnips, and ginger. A mix of some bitter or pungent veggies, such as dark leafy greens or onions, with some sweet or salty ones, such as carrot or zucchini, will yield a soup that is balancing for most doshas.

Brew Broth Stock

decreases vata, pitta, and kapha

Preparation Time: 3 hours
Yield: About 10 cups

This brew is delicious, cleansing, hearty, and flavorful. It also makes an incredibly good vegetable broth or soup stock.

2 pounds sweet potatoes
 or pumpkin, cut into 2-inch cubes

2 red onions, sliced, or more to taste

1 (3 to 4-inch) piece fresh ginger,
 peeled and sliced, or more to taste

4 to 6 cloves garlic, sliced,
 or more to taste (omit for pitta)

1 beet, cut into 2-inch cubes

1 head green cabbage, sliced

1 bunch dinosaur kale or collard
 greens, cut into 2-inch pieces

1 pound shiitake mushrooms

½ cup dried nori or sea palm

1 teaspoon salt

3 bay leaves

Put the sweet potatoes, onions, ginger, garlic, beet, and cabbage in a large stockpot with enough water to cover the vegetables. Cover. Bring to a boil over medium-high heat. Add all the remaining ingredients. Boil for 45 minutes. Decrease the heat. Simmer for 30 to 60 minutes, or until the vegetables are very soft.

Strain and discard the vegetables. Or, for a thick, creamy soup, strain out about three-quarters of the vegetables. Put the remaining vegetables in a blender or a food processor. Process until smooth, stopping occasionally to scrape down the blender jar or work bowl.

Note: This broth freezes well, so you can always have some on hand to serve as is or as a base for other soups.

Everyday Soup for All

Preparation Time: 20 minutes
Yield: 8 cups; 2 to 4 servings

The measurements here are approximate, so be bold, and cook this soup with confidence. A little more or less of each vegetable will still make this purifying, potassium-rich soup come out brilliantly, and with a lot of delicious life in it.

2 teaspoons coconut oil

3 stalks celery, chopped

1 small daikon radish or ½ medium daikon radish, chopped

2 stalks bok choy, chopped

1 small leek, minced

6 cups Brew Broth Stock (page 114) or warm water

1 large carrot, peeled and grated

1 tablespoon lemon zest

1 teaspoon salt

¼ cup minced fresh parsley

Melt the coconut oil in a large saucepan over medium heat. Add the celery, daikon, bok choy, and leek. Cook and stir for 1 minute. Add the Brew Broth Stock, carrot, lemon zest, and salt. Increase the heat to high. Cover. Cook for 5 minutes. Remove from the heat. Add the parsley. Set aside for 5 to 10 minutes before serving.

Kitchari

decreases vata, pitta, and kapha

Preparation Time: 50 minutes
Yield: 4 cups; 2 to 4 servings

A classic Indian comfort food, Kitchari is often given as an ayurvedic remedy to people who need rejuvenation from chronic exhaustion, poor digestion, or an overly toxic system. Offering warmth and spices that benefit all three doshas, Kitchari restores balance and provides vital nourishment.

½ cup white basmati rice,
    brown basmati rice or quinoa

¼ cup split yellow mung beans

1 tablespoon coconut oil

1 teaspoon cumin seeds

6 cups water

1 (1-inch) piece fresh ginger,
    peeled and minced

1 teaspoon ground cardamom

1 bay leaf

1 teaspoon ground turmeric

½ teaspoon ground cumin

½ teaspoon salt

¼ to ½ cup chopped fresh
    cilantro leaves, for garnish

1 to 2 tablespoons olive oil,
    for garnish

Rinse the rice and the beans in a fine-mesh strainer until the water runs clear. Set aside.

Melt the coconut oil in a large saucepan over medium-high heat. Add the cumin seeds. Cook and stir for 1 minute. Add the rice and beans. Cook and stir for another minute. Add the water, ginger, cardamom, and bay leaf. Bring to a boil. Cover. Decrease the heat to medium-low.

Cook for 35 to 40 minutes, stirring occasionally, or until most of the water has been absorbed. Remove the bay leaf and discard. Stir in the turmeric, ground cumin, and salt. Top each serving with 2 tablespoons of the cilantro and 1 teaspoon of the olive oil if desired.

Note: Think of Kitchari as a warm, balanced, neutral soup that you can garnish in a variety of ways for your dosha. Vata and pitta can add the juice of half a lime, while lemon would be the best choice for kapha. Everyone will benefit from 1 to 2 tablespoons of Raw Sauerkraut (page 82) on top. Both vata and kapha do well with ½ teaspoon of asafetida stirred in. You can also serve Kitchari over a bed of baby salad greens or topped with a small handful of sunflower sprouts.

Detoxification Soup

Preparation Time: 45 minutes
Yield: 4 to 6 servings

This soothing, pitta-pacifying recipe benefits the liver, gall bladder, small intestines, and spleen. Kapha will benefit from drinking this delightful soup throughout the year.

---

4 cups Brew Broth Stock (page 114), vegetable stock, or water

1 small leek, minced

½ small green cabbage, shredded

2 cups cubed, scrubbed red potatoes, or peeled and cubed acorn squash

2 cups chopped collard greens

2 cups chopped dinosaur kale

1 teaspoon cumin seeds

1 teaspoon ground ginger

¼ teaspoon salt

Juice of 1 lime or lemon

2 to 3 teaspoons olive oil, for garnish

½ cup chopped fresh parsley, for garnish

Put the Brew Broth Stock, leek, cabbage, and potatoes in a large stockpot over medium-high heat. Cover. Bring to a boil. Decrease the heat. Simmer for 15 minutes.

Add the collard greens, kale, cumin, ginger, and salt. Simmer for another 5 to 10 minutes, or until the potatoes are fork-tender. Remove from the heat. Stir in the lime juice. Drizzle each serving with ½ teaspoon of the olive oil and 1 to 2 tablespoons of the parsley if desired.

Dal

Preparation Time: 45 minutes
Yield: 6 cups

Dal soup can be ordered at almost any restaurant in India, yet I was amazed by how different it tasted in every region I traveled. Every cook seems to instinctively add a signature quality that is uniquely his own.

1 cup red lentils

1 teaspoon ground cumin

1 teaspoon ground turmeric

1 teaspoon fennel seeds

½ teaspoon ground cinnamon

½ teaspoon salt, plus more to taste

8 cups water

¼ cup toasted sea palm

½ bunch kale or
dandelion greens, chopped

4 stalks bok choy, minced

1 tablespoon miso

2 tablespoons lecithin powder

½ cup sunflower sprouts, for garnish

Put the lentils, cumin, turmeric, fennel, and cinnamon in a large, heavy saucepan over medium heat. Cook and stir for 1 minute. Add the salt, water, and sea palm. Cover. Increase the heat to medium-high. Bring to a boil. Immediately decrease the heat. Simmer for about 20 minutes, or until the lentils are soft and broken down, stirring occasionally to prevent the lentils from sticking to the pan.

Add the kale and bok choy. Simmer for another 5 minutes. Remove from the heat. Stir in the miso until it has dissolved. Sprinkle with the lecithin and salt to taste. Top each serving with the sprouts if desired.

Note: Beans and lentils are cold and dry, making them most ideal for pitta or kapha. However, soupy, well-spiced lentil soups like this serve vata well. Add 2 teaspoons of freshly grated ginger for vata and kapha. If you're in a pinch and don't have red lentils, substitute split yellow dal, split green peas, or 2 cups of cooked chickpeas.

Perfect Spring Soup

balances vata and pitta
decreases kapha

Preparation Time: 20 minutes
Yield: 6 cups; 6 servings

Light, refreshing, and tasty, this soup is for everyone to feast on in the spring. I love that it is so quick to make and yet so nutritious.

2 cups water

1 bulb fennel, chopped

2 cups chopped broccoli
   or cauliflower

1 cup chopped kale or collard greens

½ cup raw pumpkin seeds,
   sunflower seeds, or almonds

1 teaspoon coconut oil

1 small leek, chopped

2 teaspoons grated fresh ginger

2 cloves garlic, chopped
   (omit for pitta)

2 teaspoons cider vinegar
   or lemon juice

1 tablespoon miso

¼ cup chopped fresh basil
   or cilantro leaves (optional)

1 teaspoon ground cumin

1 teaspoon dried basil

½ teaspoon ground pepper

½ teaspoon salt

Place a steamer basket in a large saucepan with the water. Bring the water to a boil. Put the fennel in the steamer. Cover. Steam for 5 minutes. Add the broccoli and kale. Steam for another 5 minutes, or until the broccoli is bright green. Transfer the steamed vegetables to a colander. Set aside.

Meanwhile, put the pumpkin seeds in a food processor or blender. Process until ground. Leave them in the food processor.

Melt the coconut oil in a small skillet over medium heat. Add the leek, ginger, and garlic. Cook and stir for 5 minutes, or until the leeks are tender. Add the leek mixture, the broccoli mixture, and all the remaining ingredients to the ground seeds in the food processor. Process until smooth, stopping occasionally to scrape down the work bowl or blender jar.

Better Than Chicken Soup

decreases vata and kapha
balances pitta

Preparation Time: 30 minutes
Yield: 6 servings

Better for the planet, better for chickens, and completely awesome for all of us, this soup boosts immunity and digestive function. Eat it to strengthen your body, mind, and soul.

---

2 teaspoons coconut oil

1 teaspoon brown mustard seeds

1 teaspoon ground turmeric

1 small leek, chopped

1 (2-inch) piece fresh ginger, peeled and minced or grated

2 cloves garlic for pitta, 6 to 8 cloves garlic for vata and kapha

6 cups vegetable broth or water

2 slices dried astragalus (optional)

3 (2-inch) strips or pieces nori or kombu

2 cups peeled and cubed butternut squash

1½ cups cubed carrots and/or red potatoes

6 to 8 shiitake mushrooms, sliced

¼ bunch dinosaur kale, roughly chopped (optional)

½ teaspoon salt

⅛ teaspoon cayenne (omit for pitta)

Juice of ½ lemon (optional)

1½ tablespoons miso

Melt the coconut oil in a medium stockpot over medium-high heat. Add the mustard seeds and the turmeric. Cook and stir for 1 minute, or until the mustard seeds start to pop. Stir in the leek, ginger, and garlic. Cook for another minute. Add the broth, the optional astragalus, nori, squash, carrots, mushrooms, and optional kale. Cover and bring to a boil.

Decrease the heat to low. Simmer for 15 minutes, or until the squash is fork-tender. Remove from the heat. Remove and discard the astragalus if using. Stir in the salt, cayenne, and optional lemon juice. Cover. Set aside for 5 minutes. Stir 1 heaping teaspoon of the miso into each serving.

Note: For a more intense immune boost, make this soup with half the amount of garlic and add the other remaining raw half just before serving. Astragalus is a powerful herb commonly used in Chinese medicine to prevent immune deficiency. Tonifying and especially beneficial to the lungs and spleen, astragalus enhances the function of white blood cells that help defend the body against disease.

Steamed Collard Wraps, page 108, **with Creamy Cucumber Tahini Dressing,** page 72

red and purple potato Latkes, page 130,
with Dad's Cranberry Sauce, page 91,
and Amazing Pesto Chutney, page 74

Miso Soup

Preparation Time: 15 minutes
Yield: About 4 servings

Surprisingly tasty and with deep flavor from few ingredients, this simple soup will inspire you to say, "Bravo."

4 cups water

1 clove garlic, minced (omit for pitta)

½ teaspoon ground ginger

¼ cup toasted sea palm

¼ cup miso

2 green onions, minced

4 tablespoons Ginger, Daikon, and
   Beet Garnish (page 85) (optional)

Bring the water, garlic, and ginger to a boil in a medium saucepan over medium-high heat. Add the sea palm. Cover. Decrease the heat. Simmer for 10 minutes. Remove from the heat. Stir in the miso until most of it has dissolved. Add the green onions. Top each serving with 1 tablespoon of the Ginger, Daikon, and Beet Garnish if desired.

Raw Green Soup

Preparation Time: 15 minutes
Yield: About 4 servings

This soup is alive, refreshing, and full of alkaline-forming foods that make you feel great.

1 bunch spinach, chopped

1 bunch dinosaur kale, chopped

1 pear or apple, cored and chopped

1 avocado, chopped

Juice of 1 lemon or lime

1 (1-inch) piece fresh ginger, peeled
  and minced (omit for pitta)

½ teaspoon salt, plus more to taste

1 cup water

2 teaspoons miso (optional)

Put all the ingredients in a food processor or blender. Process until smooth and creamy, stopping occasionally to scrape down the work bowl or blender jar. Add 1 or more tablespoons of water as needed to reach the desired consistency. Season with more salt if desired.

Variations: Substitute almost any green vegetables for the spinach and kale in this recipe. Different greens will yield different flavors, colors, and vitamins. In varying combinations, ½ bunch of collard greens, celery, dill weed, or bok choy, 1 small zucchini, 1 bunch of watercress, and ¼ bunch of mustard greens can all be substituted in this recipe.

For vata, lightly steam the spinach and kale before combining them with the other ingredients and substitute Fresh Ginger Tea (page 35) for the water.

Curried Ginger–Squash Soup

Preparation Time: 50 minutes
Yield: 4 to 6 servings

This satisfying soup helps us stay grounded, warm, and rooted in the cool autumn chill. It's made with just the right amount of spice.

---

3 cups water

1 small pumpkin or 1 butternut squash, unpeeled, cut into 2-inch chunks

1 cup chopped leek or red onion

3 cloves garlic, minced

1 (2-inch) piece fresh ginger, peeled and minced

1 apple, cored and diced

1 teaspoon green curry paste, or 1 small jalapeño chile, minced

2 tablespoons maple syrup

2 tablespoons olive oil

2 tablespoons tamari, Bragg Liquid Aminos, or coconut aminos

1 teaspoon ground cinnamon

1 teaspoon ground turmeric

1 teaspoon ground coriander

½ teaspoon cumin seeds

½ teaspoon ground pepper

½ teaspoon salt

Place a steamer basket in a large pot with the water. Bring the water to a boil. Put the pumpkin in the steamer basket. Cover. Steam for 15 minutes, or until the pumpkin is fork-tender. Transfer the pumpkin to a colander. Set aside. Remove the steamer basket from the pot.

Put the leek, garlic, ginger, apple, and curry paste in the pot of hot steam water. Cover. Set aside. Rinse the steamed pumpkin under cold running water until it is cool enough to handle. Remove the peel. Put the pumpkin flesh, the leek mixture, and all the remaining ingredients in a food processor or blender. (You may have to do this in batches.) Process until smooth, stopping occasionally to scrape down the work bowl.

Note: For kapha, substitute half of a sweet potato and half of a parsnip or celery root for the pumpkin.

CHAPTER 11
Side Dishes

I AM A HUGE FAN OF SIDE DISHES. I like to have my food flavorful, diverse, and—to be honest—exactly how I want it. Side dishes help balance meals so you can fine-tune them to your specific dosha. Plus, it's easy to mix and match a variety of sides and create choice combinations of flavor that double as protein-boosters and/ or quick nutritional enhancements to simple salads, grains, soups, and vegetables.

The stars of this chapter are some of my all-time favorites, and I'm confident you will enjoy them, too. Many of the recipes in this section make great main meal attractions, or they can serve as accompaniments to the other sides you'll find here.

An ample amount of the side dishes that follow include beans or grains. In order to apply your skill to the test of food combining, it's helpful to know which beans and grains are most balancing for your dosha. Use the following list to determine which recipes will please your body, mind, and spirit the most.

Beans and Grains that Balance Vata
Adzuki, amaranth, black beans, black rice, brown rice, mung beans, oats, red lentils, red rice, spicy tofu, sweet rice, and tempeh

Beans and Grains that Balance Pitta
Adzuki, basmati rice, black beans, chickpeas, jade rice, kidney beans, mung beans, split peas, tofu, and white rice

Beans and Grains that Balance Kapha
Adzuki, barley, black beans, brown basmati rice, buckwheat, chickpeas, millet, mung beans, quinoa, red lentils, rye, split peas, spicy tofu, and tempeh, in moderation

Baked Tempeh

decreases vata
increases pitta
balances kapha

Preparation Time: 40 minutes
Yield: 2 servings

Fermented soybeans, in the form of miso and tempeh, are easier to digest than tofu or soy milk and offer a good amount of protein. This steamed-then-baked version serves up a tempeh that is plump, slightly crisp, and oh, so delicious. I love it tossed into salads and bowls of steaming whole grains.

---

1 (8-ounce) package tempeh

2 tablespoons coconut oil

2 tablespoons tamari, Bragg Liquid Aminos, or coconut aminos

2 tablespoons water

½ teaspoon salt

2 teaspoons nutritional yeast flakes

1 teaspoon ground cumin

1 teaspoon herbes de Provence

Preheat the oven to 350 degrees F. Slice the tempeh into ½-inch cubes. Or, if you arc making Tempeh Reuben (page 105), slice the tempeh in half crosswise. Stand each slice on end and cut each slice in half through the middle to make 4 thin slices. Cut each thin slice in half diagonally to make 8 triangular pieces.

Melt the coconut oil in a large, shallow skillet over medium heat. Put the tempeh in the skillet. Drizzle it with the tamari and water. Sprinkle it with the salt, nutritional yeast, cumin, and herbes de Provence. Cover. Cook for 10 to 15 minutes, or until all the liquid has evaporated. Stir a few times to prevent the tempeh from sticking to the pan. Be careful not to break the tempeh slices.

Transfer the tempeh to a baking dish in a single layer. Bake for 10 to 15 minutes, or until golden brown.

Savory Soup Cookies

Preparation Time: 45 minutes
Yield: 2 dozen cookies

These are a scrumptious alternative to bread, make great savory breakfast scones, and are an epic side dish to steaming bowls of homemade soup.

1½ cups brown rice flour

1 cup chickpea flour
   or amaranth flour

1 cup tapioca flour

1 teaspoon baking powder

1 teaspoon baking soda

2 teaspoons xanthan gum
   or tapioca flour

½ teaspoon salt

½ cup plus 1 teaspoon
   melted coconut oil

1 small red onion, chopped

2 teaspoons dried sage

½ teaspoon brown mustard seeds

⅔ cup maple syrup
   or raw agave nectar

½ cup Almond Milk (page 34)
   or prepared almond milk,
   plus more as needed

1 teaspoon cider vinegar

1 teaspoon vanilla extract

Preheat the oven to 375 degrees F. Sift the brown rice flour, chickpea flour, tapioca flour, baking powder, baking soda, xanthan gum, and salt into a large bowl. Set aside.

Melt 1 teaspoon of the coconut oil in a small skillet over medium-low heat. Add the onion, sage, and mustard seeds. Cook and stir for 2 or 3 minutes, or until the onion is slightly soft and the mustard seeds start to pop. Transfer to a separate large bowl. Stir in the maple syrup, the remaining ½ cup of the coconut oil, the Almond Milk, vinegar, and vanilla extract. Add the flour mixture 1 cup at a time, mixing thoroughly after each addition. If the dough is too thick, add the Almond Milk 1 teaspoon at a time until all of the flour mixture can be incorporated.

With wet hands, form the dough into 2- to 3-inch biscuits. Place them 2 inches apart on a large baking sheet. Bake for 15 to 20 minutes, or until the cookies form a thin, golden crust and a toothpick inserted into the centers comes out clean. Let cool for 5 minutes before serving.

Ayurvedic Brown Rice

balances vata
decreases pitta and kapha

Preparation Time: 45 minutes
Yield: 2 to 4 servings

This rice is simple, cleansing, easy to prepare, and good for building strong digestive fire. The spices used here—fennel, cumin and coriander—are digestive regulators that balance all three doshas.

---

1 cup brown rice

1 teaspoon salt

1 tablespoon fennel seeds

2 teaspoons ground cumin

2 teaspoons ground coriander

2 cups water

Put the rice, salt, fennel, cumin, and coriander in a medium, heavy saucepan over medium heat. Cook for 1 minute, or until the mixture is very aromatic, stirring constantly. Add the water. Cover. Bring to a boil. Decrease the heat. Simmer for 35 to 40 minutes, or until all of the water has been absorbed.

Note: There are so many beautiful types of rice being cultivated throughout the world. I urge you to try them when you have the opportunity. Darker grains, such as Japanese black rice, are high in protein, rich in minerals, and very good for the kidneys and urinary system. Substitute heirloom rice varieties, such as Bhutanese Red Rice and Jade Rice, for brown rice in this recipe. Cooking times may vary for different rice varieties, so take note of the package directions before cooking them.

Fried Soup Onions

Preparation Time: 10 minutes
Yield: ¾ cup; 4 servings

These onions taste great and motivate cool, moist kapha. Serve them on top of Kitchari (page 116) or Raw Green Soup (page 122).

1 teaspoon coconut oil

½ teaspoon brown mustard seeds

½ teaspoon fennel seeds

½ teaspoon cumin seeds

1 red or yellow onion,
   cut into ⅛-inch slices

1 clove garlic, minced (omit for pitta)

¼ teaspoon salt

¼ teaspoon ground turmeric
   or curry powder (optional)

½ teaspoon brown rice syrup
   or raw agave nectar (optional)

Preheat the oven to 400 degrees F. Melt the coconut oil in a medium skillet over medium-high heat. Add the mustard seeds, fennel, and cumin. When the seeds start to pop, add the onion and garlic. Cook and stir until the onion is soft and translucent, about 5 minutes. Remove from the heat. Stir in the salt and the optional turmeric and brown rice syrup.

Spread the onion mixture on a medium rimmed baking sheet. Bake for 5 minutes, stirring every 2 minutes to prevent the onions from burning. Use as a garnish over soups, stews, and grain dishes.

Latkes

Preparation Time: 40 minutes
Yield: 12 pancakes; 6 servings

SEE PHOTO FACING PAGE 121.

We used to make salty, oily versions of latkes in my Hebrew school days. Now, these traditional crispy pancakes are back, with a more healthful attitude.

---

6 red or purple potatoes, scrubbed

1 large red onion, minced

1 teaspoon cumin seeds

½ teaspoon ground cumin or turmeric

½ teaspoon ground nutmeg or mace

1 tablespoon egg replacer

4 tablespoons water

½ cup amaranth flour

½ teaspoon baking powder

1 teaspoon salt

2 or 3 tablespoons coconut oil

Grate the potatoes on the large-hole side of a box grater into a colander. Rinse and drain. Press on the potatoes with a dish towel to squeeze out as much liquid as possible. Transfer the potatoes to a large bowl. Stir in the onion, cumin seeds, ground cumin, and nutmeg.

Whisk the egg replacer with the water in a small bowl until smooth. Add it to the potato mixture, along with the flour, baking powder, and salt.

Preheat the oven to 250 degrees F. Place a large baking sheet and a plate lined with a stack of paper towels or dish towels nearby to drain the latkes after cooking.

Melt 2 tablespoons of the coconut oil in a large skillet over medium-high heat until very hot. (The skillet should be hot enough so that a drop of batter sizzles.) Drop 3 to 4 tablespoons of the batter into the skillet for each latke. Fry until brown and crispy, about 2 minutes. Turn the latke over. Fry the other side until brown and crispy, about another 2 minutes. Add the coconut oil to the pan as needed.

Transfer each latke to the prepared plate to drain. Transfer drained latkes to the baking sheet. Place them in the oven to keep them warm until ready to serve. Repeat with the remaining batter.

Note: It's traditional to serve latkes with homemade applesauce at Hanukkah time, but why not do something a little unconventional? Try Latkes with Amazing Pesto Chutney (page 74) and Dad's Cranberry Sauce (page 91) for a savory twist.

Stuffed Mushroom Caps

increases vata
slightly decreases pitta and kapha

Preparation Time: 30 minutes
Yield: 24 mushroom caps; about 5 servings

The first word that comes to mind is "yum." The second is "easy." Stuffed Mushroom Caps make an amazingly delicious appetizer or a great meal, when paired with a salad or a steaming bowl of quinoa.

---

24 medium to large cremini mushrooms

2 slices brown rice bread or bread of your choice

½ cup raw almonds

½ cup minced kale, dandelion greens, or bok choy

¼ cup Amazing Pesto Chutney (page 74) or prepared vegan pesto

2 cloves garlic, minced (omit for pitta)

½ teaspoon ground turmeric

½ teaspoon salt

2 or 3 tablespoons olive oil (optional)

2 tablespoons Palmesan Cheese (page 90) or prepared vegan Parmesan, for garnish

1 teaspoon fresh dill weed, for garnish

Preheat the oven to 350 degrees F. Remove the mushroom stems and set aside.

Toast the bread in a toaster until crispy and golden brown. Let cool for 2 minutes. Crumble the bread into a blender or food processor. Process until it forms coarse crumbs. Add the almonds to the food processor with the bread crumbs. Process about 10 seconds, or until the almonds are coarsely ground.

Add the kale, reserved mushroom stems, Amazing Pesto Chutney, garlic, turmeric, and salt to the food processor. Process until well combined, stopping occasionally to scrape down the work bowl. The texture will be slightly coarse. Add the optional oil for a thicker, creamier paste.

Stuff each mushroom cap with about 2 teaspoons of the filling. Place the stuffed mushroom caps in a 13 x 9-inch baking pan. Pour 1 cup of water into a separate baking pan. Place it on the lower rack of the oven. Place the pan of stuffed mushroom caps on the top or middle rack of the oven. Bake for 15 to 20 minutes, or until the mushrooms are moist and brown. Sprinkle the stuffed mushrooms with the Palmesan Cheese and dill before serving if desired.

Stuffed Mushroom Pizzas
(decreases vata, pitta, and kapha): Substitute 4 medium to large portobello mushrooms for the creminis. Stuff each portobello mushroom with ¼ cup of the filling. Top each stuffed mushroom with 2 teaspoons of chopped, oil-soaked, sun-dried tomatoes and ¼ teaspoon of minced garlic (omit the garlic for pitta). Bake for 30 minutes. Garnish with Palmesan Cheese and dill before serving if desired.

Broccoli with Miso Sauce

increases vata slightly
decreases pitta and kapha

Preparation Time: 15 minutes
Yield: 4 to 6 servings

Overcooking antioxidant-rich broccoli will deplete its amazing health benefits, so cook it only until bright green and firm. It will thank you by fortifying your blood, heart, bones, and eyes.

4 cups chopped broccoli florets

1 heaping tablespoon miso

2 teaspoons hot water,
  plus more as needed

2 tablespoons Vegan Mayonnaise
  (page 75) or prepared vegan
  mayonnaise

1 tablespoon raw agave nectar
  or maple syrup

1 teaspoon caraway seeds
  or cumin seeds

½ teaspoon curry powder

½ teaspoon fresh dill weed

½ cup mung bean sprouts,
  for garnish

Place a steamer basket in a stockpot with 1 cup of water. Bring the water to a boil. Put the broccoli in the steamer. Steam about 5 minutes, or just until the broccoli turns bright green and is still firm. Transfer the broccoli to a colander. Set aside.

Combine the miso with the hot water in a small bowl until the miso has dissolved. Stir in the Vegan Mayonnaise, agave nectar, caraway, curry powder, and dill weed until creamy. Add another 1 or 2 tablespoons of hot water if it seems too thick. Pour the dressing over the broccoli. Garnish with the sprouts if desired.

Steamed Cabbage and Apples

increases vata
decreases pitta and kapha

Preparation Time: 20 minutes
Yield: 4 cups; 4 servings

One of the best-loved collaborations between my adventurous, food-loving cousin and me, circa 1993, this version has been updated to reflect modern times. It's yummy on its own, or with a bowl of plain brown rice, oatmeal, or quinoa.

1 cup water

½ small red cabbage, minced

1 green apple, cored and cut into ½-inch cubes

¼ cup slivered almonds

2 tablespoons coconut sugar or dehydrated cane juice

2 teaspoons sesame seeds or flaxseeds

½ teaspoon ground cinnamon

Place a steamer basket in a medium saucepan with the water. Bring the water to a boil. Put the cabbage in the steamer basket. Cover. Steam for 4 minutes. Add the apple. Steam for another 2 minutes, or until the cabbage and apples are slightly soft.

Transfer the cabbage and apples to a medium bowl. Add all the remaining ingredients. Toss to combine.

Note: Vata can increase the amount of cinnamon, and maybe add a dash of mace, cloves, or cardamom. Top with 1 teaspoon of sesame oil.

Vegan Paneer Cheese

balances vata and pitta
increases kapha

Preparation Time: 1 hour (cooked); 25 hours (raw)
Yield: 2 cups

Paneer is a traditional, soft-curd cheese used in Indian cooking. Here are two versions, one cooked and one raw, of delectable vegan paneer.

Cooked paneer

- 1 (14–ounce) package organic firm tofu
- 2 tablespoons Almond Milk (page 34), Rice Milk (page 34), or prepared almond, rice or hempseed milk
- 1 tablespoon nutritional yeast flakes or lecithin powder
- 1 teaspoon stone-ground mustard
- 1 teaspoon onion powder
- ½ teaspoon salt
- ¼ teaspoon ground turmeric (optional)
- ¼ teaspoon brown mustard seeds (optional)
- 2 teaspoons coconut oil

To squeeze out the excess moisture from the tofu, place the tofu on a clean, double-folded dish towel on the countertop. Place another clean, double-folded dish towel on top of the tofu. Place a heavy cutting board on top. Place another heavy object, such as a bowl, on top of the cutting board. Set aside for 15 to 20 minutes.

Meanwhile, stir the Almond Milk, nutritional yeast, mustard, onion powder, salt, and the optional turmeric and mustard seeds in a small bowl until creamy. Put the tofu in a small baking pan. Pour the almond milk mixture over the tofu. Let it marinate in the refrigerator for 20 minutes.

Cut the tofu into ½-inch cubes. Melt the coconut oil in a large, heavy skillet over medium heat. Put the tofu and the marinade in the skillet. Cook and stir 3 to 5 minutes, or until the tofu is golden brown. Stored in a tightly covered container in the refrigerator, cooked Vegan Paneer Cheese will keep for 5 days.

Note: Pressing tofu results in an extra-firm texture that absorbs more flavor when cooked. Use pressed tofu when cooking with tofu in stir-fries.

Raw paneer

**2 cups raw macadamia nuts
or cashews**

1 cup water

**1 teaspoon rejuvelac, or ½ teaspoon
powdered probiotic (optional)**

1 teaspoon salt

1 tablespoon nutritional yeast flakes

Line a fine-mesh strainer with cheesecloth. Place it over a large bowl. Put the macadamia nuts, water, and optional rejuvelac in a blender. Process until smooth, stopping occasionally to scrape down the blender jar. Pour the macadamia mixture into the prepared strainer. Cover with another piece of cheesecloth or a dish towel. Place a weight, such as a heavy bowl, on top of the mixture to press out the excess liquid. Set aside for 24 hours at room temperature.

Transfer the pressed mixture to a medium bowl. With a spoon, stir in the salt and nutritional yeast. Spread the mixture in a ½-inch layer in an 11 x 8-inch glass baking pan. Cover. Refrigerate for 1 hour. Cut the vegan paneer into ½-inch cubes. Stored in a tightly covered container in the refrigerator, raw Vegan Paneer Cheese will keep for 1 week.

Note: Do not cook this raw nut cheese. Rather, add it to stir-fries and other dishes at the end of cooking, as a garnish, or as a last-minute addition.

Spinach Pie

Preparation Time: 30 minutes
Yield: 1 (10-inch) pie; 4 to 6 servings

Serve Spinach Pie as a gluten-free flatbread alongside soups and salads, or pair it with the filling for Thankful Pie (page 162). It's a surprisingly savory way to get your greens.

---

1 tablespoon coconut oil

1 cup minced leek

½ teaspoon salt

½ teaspoon cumin seeds

2 cups chopped spinach,
   tightly packed

2 cups chopped Swiss chard,
   tightly packed

¼ cup raw almonds, Brazil nuts,
   or pine nuts

¾ cup brown rice flour

1 teaspoon sesame seeds

½ teaspoon ground nutmeg

⅛ teaspoon ground cardamom
   (optional)

Preheat the oven to 350 degrees F. Oil the bottom of a 10-inch glass pie pan with coconut oil. Set aside.

Melt the coconut oil in a large, heavy skillet over medium-high heat. Add the leek, salt, and cumin. Cook and stir for 1 minute. Stir in the spinach and chard. Cook until wilted, about 2 minutes. Remove from the heat.

Put the almonds in a blender or food processor. Process to a fine meal. Combine the almond meal, brown rice flour, sesame seeds, nutmeg, and optional cardamom in a medium bowl. Add the spinach mixture to the flour mixture and combine. Press the mixture into the prepared pan. Bake for 12 to 15 minutes. Let cool before serving.

Note: Substitute any of your favorite dark, leafy greens for the spinach and Swiss chard. Bok choy, mustard greens, and dinosaur kale are particularly good.

Herbed Millet

Preparation Time: 30 minutes
Yield: 4 servings

Simple, light, and hearty, Herbed Millet is a versatile, savory dish that pairs well with Amazing Pesto Chutney (page 74) or Tahini-Miso Dressing (page 71). I also like to top it with Fried Soup Onions (page 129). Yum.

1 cup millet

2¼ cups water or vegetable broth

1 teaspoon olive oil

1 teaspoon salt

1 teaspoon ground cumin

½ cup chopped fresh dill weed

Pour the millet into a fine-mesh strainer. Rinse and drain. Transfer the millet, water, oil, and salt to a medium saucepan over medium-high heat. Bring to a boil. Decrease the heat. Cover. Simmer for 20 minutes, or until all the water has been absorbed. Remove from the heat. Set aside, covered, for 5 minutes. Fluff with a fork. Stir in the cumin and dill.

Banana Commitment Curry

Preparation Time: 20 minutes

Yield: About 2 cups

When I was done with the idea of waiting for somebody else to choose me, I decided to be "the one" and commit to myself. I invited about 50 guests, wore a vintage wedding dress, walked down the aisle, and read my own vows. This side dish, brought by a guest, remains one of my fondest memories from that totally perfect day.

---

1 tablespoon coconut oil

1½ teaspoons ground turmeric

1 teaspoon ground cumin

5 firm bananas, cut into
   1-inch chunks

1 teaspoon salt

2 teaspoons curry powder

2 tablespoons water

1 cup coconut yogurt or
   other vegan yogurt or Creamy
   Coconut Kefir (page 44)

1 teaspoon ground cardamom

⅛ teaspoon cayenne

Juice of 1 lemon

Melt the coconut oil in a large, heavy skillet over medium heat. Stir in the turmeric and cumin. Cook for 1 minute. Add the bananas, salt, and curry powder. Cook for 5 minutes, stirring constantly to prevent the bananas from sticking to the pan.

Add the water. Cook for another 5 minutes. Decrease the heat to low. Stir in the yogurt, cardamom, cayenne, and lemon juice. Simmer for 5 minutes, stirring constantly. Serve warm.

Note: Banana Commitment Curry is fabulous over rice, quinoa, or almost any combination of steamed vegetables.

CHAPTER 12
Snacks

THESE RECIPES ARE GREAT WHEN YOU ARE TRAVELING, on the go, or hungry between meals. You can incorporate them into your daily diet as condiments or complementary side dishes. Some will satisfy a sweet tooth, with just the right amount of protein to keep you feeling good.

It's important to have healthful snacks on hand so blood sugar levels don't drop. When blood sugar is unbalanced, vata feels weak, pitta gets irritated, and kapha may overeat.

When in doubt, soaked nuts and seeds are an easy, protein-rich snack at any time. They ferment fast, so if you're not planning to eat them right away, soak only the amount that you plan to eat within a few days, and keep them in the refrigerator. Soaked nuts and seeds can also be sprinkled on salads, whole grains, and steamed vegetables.

Snacks that Balance Vata
Skinless almonds, fresh apricots, avocados, bananas, cherries, coconut, dates, figs, grapefruit, spicy kale chips, kiwifruit, mangoes, mulberries, papayas, peaches, pineapple, plums, soaked raisins, raw food bars, and strawberries

Snacks that Balance Pitta
Soaked and dehydrated almonds, apples, apricots, blueberries, coconut, dates, figs, grapes, kale chips, mangoes, oranges, pears, plums, pomegranates, raspberries, raw food bars, raw granola, raw seed breads, raw trail mixes, crunchy sea vegetable snacks, and watermelon

Snacks that Balance Kapha
Apples, blackberries, cherries, dried figs, flaxseed crackers, kale chips, raw granola, pears, peaches, raw pumpkin seeds, raisins, rice cakes, and watermelon

Toasted Wild Nori Snack

balances vata, pitta, and kapha

Preparation Time: 10 minutes
Yield: 1 cup

Toasted nori is a satisfying salty snack packed with protein, chlorophyll, vitamins, and a yummy crunch. Eat it straight out of the oven, or crumble it over salads, whole grains, and soups.

---

1 cup raw, wild nori, packed

Preheat the oven to 300 degrees F. Spread the nori on a baking sheet. Bake about 10 minutes, or until crisp.

Spirulinafied

balances vata, pitta, and kapha

Preparation Time: 15 minutes
Yield: 4 servings

It is my personal opinion that fresh, sweet pineapple dipped in spirulina is a sattvic food. Pineapple creates healthful digestive fire, and spirulina balances pineapple's acidity with cool, oxygenating chlorophyll and blood sugar-balancing protein. The flavors meld perfectly.

---

2 tablespoons spirulina

1 ripe fresh pineapple, cored, peeled, and cut into 1-inch chunks

Pour the spirulina into a small bowl. Dip the pineapple chunks into the spirulina until well coated.

Notes: A fresh pineapple is ripe when it smells sweet, its skin is a mostly golden-yellow color, and it is relatively firm to the touch. For a truly delicious experience, I recommend using Spirulina Manna by Healthforce Nutritionals. Spirulina also tastes amazing with fresh, juicy strawberries or mango spears.

Stewed Prunes and Apricots

balances vata
decreases pitta and kapha

Preparation Time: 15 minutes
Yield: About 2 cups

Sweet cooked fruits are great for kapha (in moderation) and provide fast, grounding, iron-rich nourishment for vata and pitta. Try this with Creamy Coconut Kefir (page 44) or on top of Oat Groats Cereal (page 48).

---

1 cup dried pitted prunes

1 cup dried apricots (preferably Turkish)

1 tablespoon fennel seeds

4 cups water

1 orange, sliced thin (optional)

Put all the ingredients in a medium saucepan over medium-high heat. Cover. Bring to a boil. Decrease the heat to low. Simmer for 10 minutes. Let cool. Stored in a covered container in the refrigerator, Stewed Prunes and Apricots will keep for 7 to 10 days.

Sauerkraut Toasts

decreases vata and pitta
balances kapha

Preparation Time: 10 minutes
Yield: 1 to 2 servings

If you think you don't like sauerkraut, I dare you to try this. Something about the combination of raw seed or nut butter and sauerkraut is just right. Thank you to my ayurvedic sisters for inspiring this fast and delicious recipe.

---

1 slice sprouted-grain bread or brown rice bread (see Note)

1 heaping tablespoon raw tahini or raw almond butter

1 to 2 tablespoons Raw Sauerkraut (page 82) or prepared raw sauerkraut

½ teaspoon ground coriander (optional)

2 tablespoons sunflower sprouts or alfalfa sprouts

Toast the bread in a toaster until golden brown. Spread the toast with tahini. Top with the Raw Sauerkraut, sprinkle with the optional coriander, and top with the sprouts.

Note: Vata and kapha, or those with sensitive or weak digestive systems, may find sprouted-grain bread easier to digest than regular flour-based bread.

Goddess Trail Mix

Preparation Time: 5 minutes
Yield: 2 cups

This is a yummy snack or topping for creamy desserts, vegan yogurt, Creamy Coconut Kefir (page 44), and hot, whole-grain cereals.

---

1 cup raw pine nuts

¾ cup crystallized ginger,
  cubed or diced

¾ cup goji berries

½ cup raw cacao nibs

Combine all the ingredients in a bowl.

Oil and Vinegar Potato Chips

Preparation Time: 5 minutes
Yield: About 1 cup; 2 servings

Raw red potatoes are a magnificent cleansing food. Their cool, astringent properties serve all doshas, but like most raw foods, vata should enjoy these chips in moderation.

---

2 red potatoes, scrubbed and
  cut into 1/8-inch slices

1 teaspoon coconut vinegar
  or cider vinegar

¼ teaspoon salt

½ teaspoon dried basil
  (optional)

⅛ teaspoon ground pepper

Put the potatoes in a medium bowl. Pour the vinegar over the potatoes and sprinkle them with the salt, optional basil, and pepper. Toss to mix well.

CHAPTER 13
Desserts

Sweets are something special, an offering of love.
— **Amadea Morningstar**

DESSERTS COME FROM THE HEART, especially when they are prepared with mindfulness, nutritional know-how, and a desire to serve great-tasting food with loving care.

Kapha types embody the very nature of sweetness, both in physical form and in their sweet and generous dispositions. An overindulgence in sweet taste will unbalance kapha immediately. Sweet is best for vata and pitta but will still unbalance them when eaten in excess.

Desserts were the sole reason for my decision to become an ayurvedic chef. I had to find a way to include them in my life while tending to my health and wellness. The recipes in this section are my precious babies. I hope you love them as much as I do.

Sweeteners Best for Vata
Brown rice syrup, dates, dehydrated cane juice, jaggery, maple syrup, and molasses

Sweeteners Best for Pitta
Brown rice syrup, coconut nectar, dates, frozen fruit juice concentrate, maple syrup, and sweet fruits

Sweeteners Best for Kapha
Raw agave nectar, coconut nectar, dried fruits, frozen fruit juice concentrate, Jerusalem artichoke syrup, and raw yacon syrup

Berry Kapha Pie

balances vata, pitta, and kapha

Preparation Time: 35 minutes
Yield: 1 (9-inch) pie; 6 to 8 servings

Most desserts can unbalance kapha, but this pie is simple, light, and fresh, three of the best qualities kapha can find in a dessert. Make it in winter months with the frozen fresh fruit you saved at fall harvest time (hint, hint).

Crust

1 tablespoon coconut oil

1 cup vegan granola

¼ cup raw almonds

2 teaspoons flaxseeds

½ teaspoon fennel seeds (optional)

Filling

1 cup ½-inch slices peaches, nectarines, apricots, pears, or figs

2 cups strawberries, blackberries, olallieberries, or blueberries

2 tablespoons coconut sugar or dehydrated cane juice

2 teaspoons arrowroot starch or brown rice flour

Juice of ½ lemon

1 teaspoon ground cardamom

½ teaspoon ground cinnamon

To make the crust, preheat the oven to 350 degrees F. To melt the coconut oil, place the container on the warm stovetop for a few minutes, or in a bowl of hot water for 1 minute. Oil a 9-inch glass pie pan with 1 teaspoon of the coconut oil. Set aside.

Put the granola, almonds, flaxseeds, and optional fennel seeds in a food processor or blender. Process until ground to a coarse meal. Add the remaining 2 teaspoons of the coconut oil and process again. Transfer the crust mixture into the prepared pie pan. Press the mixture evenly into the bottom and up the sides of the pan.

To make the filling, mix the peaches, strawberries, sugar, arrowroot, lemon juice, cardamom, and cinnamon in a medium bowl. Transfer the filling into the prepared crust. Bake for 15 minutes.

Note: Keep kapha balanced by using seasonal fruits in this pie, such as berries in the spring, peaches in the summer, fresh figs in the fall, and pears in the winter.

Healthful Homemade Halvah balances vata, pitta, and kapha

Preparation Time: 5 minutes
Yield: About 1 cup

When I spent some time traveling through Israel, I became addicted to this malty, sweet confection. Now I make it from scratch—and pray for peace.

½ cup raw tahini
  or raw cashew butter

2 heaping tablespoons softened
  coconut butter (optional)

¼ cup maple syrup

Put all the ingredients in a blender. Process until smooth, stopping occasionally to scrape down the blender jar. Pour into serving dishes. Store in a sealed container in the refrigerator.

Marbled Halvah
(balances vata and kapha, increases pitta slightly): Pour half of the halvah batter into a bowl. Mix in 1 teaspoon of raw cacao powder or raw carob powder. Swirl the chocolate halvah batter through the plain halvah.

Indian Fennel Candy balances vata, pitta, and kapha

Preparation Time: 10 minutes
Yield: About ½ cup

You'll find a candy like this offered in many Indian restaurants and temples as you enter, which always feels very heartfelt and welcoming to me. Use it to kindle digestive fire, before or after a meal.

½ cup fennel seeds

2 tablespoons cumin seeds

2 tablespoons coriander seeds

2 tablespoons crumbled jaggery
  or coconut sugar

⅛ teaspoon ground cardamom

Pour the fennel, cumin, and coriander into a heavy skillet over medium heat. Gently dry roast the seeds, stirring constantly, until aromatic. Remove from the heat. Stir in the jaggery and the cardamom. Store in a glass candy jar.

Almond Dream Cream

Preparation Time: 10 minutes, plus overnight soaking time
Yield: 2 cups

I love to eat this ambrosial cream with fresh berries or as a topping over Sandy Lane Cherry Pie (page 163). It also makes a great cream base for shakes and smoothies.

1 cup raw almonds

5 cups water

3 medjool dates, or 3 tablespoons
   Date Paste (see Note)

1 teaspoon vanilla extract

1 teaspoon maple syrup
   or brown rice syrup

Soak the almonds overnight in 3 cups of the water. Drain and rinse. Transfer the almonds to a food processor with 2 cups of fresh water. Add all the remaining ingredients. Process for 20 seconds, or until smooth, stopping occasionally to scrape down the work bowl. Stored in a covered glass jar in the refrigerator, Almond Dream Cream will keep for 3 to 5 days.

Frozen Almond Dream Cream
(balances vata and kapha, decreases pitta): Strain the Almond Dream Cream in a fine-mesh strainer lined with a double layer of cheesecloth. Transfer to a covered container and freeze. Serve with the brown rice syrup as a yummy dessert.

Date Paste: Put 4 pitted, medjool dates in a blender or a food processor. Process for about 5 seconds. If dates seem dry, add ½ teaspoon of water. Alternatively, mash them with a mortar and pestle. Four large dates will yield approximately ¼ cup of date paste.

Chai-Chocolate Mousse

decreases vata and pitta
balances kapha

Preparation Time: 10 minutes, plus 30-minute soak time
Yield: 2 cups

I went to Hebrew school with one of America's best-selling raw food cookbook authors, Jennifer Cornbleet. If you don't have her first cookbook, Raw Food Made Easy for 1 or 2 People, get a copy of it pronto. There's a reason why it's a bestseller, and the inspiration for this recipe is one of them.

¾ cup Chai (page 32)
  or prepared chai

½ cup medjool dates, pitted

½ cup maple syrup

1 teaspoon vanilla extract

2½ avocados

1 (1-inch) piece fresh ginger, chopped

¾ cup raw carob powder
  or raw cacao powder

1 teaspoon ground cinnamon

1 teaspoon ground cardamom

2 tablespoons raw cacao nibs
  (optional)

Prepare the Chai. Let cool to room temperature or refrigerate for 1 to 2 hours. Soak the dates in water to cover in a small bowl for 30 minutes. Drain.

Put the dates, maple syrup, ¼ cup of the Chai, and the vanilla extract in a food processor or blender. Process until smooth, stopping occasionally to scrape down the work bowl or blender jar. Add the avocados, ginger, carob powder, cinnamon, and cardamom. Process until creamy. Add the remaining Chai and process again briefly. Serve in small bowls. Sprinkle with the optional cacao nibs.

Note: The reserved date soak water is nourishing to vata and pitta. Dates are known to strengthen the liver when taken in moderation, and can be used as a general tonifying treat.

Marzipan Truffles

Preparation Time: 20 minutes
Yield: 18 truffles

I came up with this recipe especially for my dearest friend, Gwendolyn. She loves marzipan and is always looking for one that is healthful and balanced. Gwendolyn, my love, this one's for you.

¾ cup raw sugar

1 cup water, plus more as needed

2½ cups ground almonds

⅛ teaspoon nutmeg (optional)

¼ cup coconut oil

½ cup raw cacao powder

2 tablespoons maple syrup
  or coconut nectar

1 teaspoon vanilla extract

Bring the sugar and ½ cup of the water to a boil in a large saucepan over high heat. Boil for 5 minutes, stirring constantly, until syrupy. Decrease the heat to low. Stir in the almonds and optional nutmeg. The mixture should be sticky. If it isn't sticky, add 1 tablespoon of water. Transfer the mixture to a bowl. Let cool for about 10 minutes. Roll the mixture into 1-inch balls with your hands. Set aside on a plate.

To make the chocolate truffle coating, bring the remaining ½ cup of water to a boil in a small saucepan over medium-high heat. Put the coconut oil in a small glass measuring cup. Place the measuring cup in the boiling water until the coconut oil melts. Pour the coconut oil into a medium bowl. Add the cacao powder, maple syrup, and vanilla extract. Stir well.

Dip each marzipan ball into the chocolate mixture to cover one half of each truffle with chocolate. Place them on a serving plate. Refrigerate the truffles for 10 minutes before serving. Stored in a covered container in the refrigerator, Marzipan Truffles will keep for 3 weeks.

Decadent Baked Apples

balances vata
decreases pitta and kapha

Preparation Time: 1 hour
Yield: 4 servings

Nothing makes you feel cozy in autumn like a simple dessert of baked apples. Make them for friends and family and give thanks for life.

4 medium to large apples
or pears, cored

8 dried figs, chopped

⅓ cup coarsely chopped raw almonds

½ cup raisins or currants

¼ cup raw sunflower seeds

2 tablespoons minced
crystallized ginger (optional)

1 tablespoon ground cinnamon

1 teaspoon ground nutmeg

1 teaspoon ground cardamom

1 teaspoon lemon zest

1 tablespoon brown rice
syrup (optional)

2 cups unfiltered apple juice
or pear juice

4 teaspoons softened coconut
butter (optional)

Preheat the oven to 350 degrees F. Place the apples in an 8 x 8-inch glass baking pan. Set aside.

Mix the figs, almonds, raisins, sunflower seeds, optional ginger, cinnamon, nutmeg, cardamom, lemon zest, and optional brown rice syrup in a medium bowl. Fill the cores of the apples with the fig mixture. Scatter the remaining fig mixture over the top of the apples. Pour the juice over them. Bake for 45 minutes. Top each baked apple with a teaspoon of the optional coconut butter before serving.

Dadus

Preparation time: 30 minutes
Yield: About 30 balls

SEE PHOTO FACING PAGE 152.

*The Sanskrit word for ball is **ladu** (pronounced LAH-doo) and specifically refers to sweets. I had been making these little cookies for my uncle because he loved them, but I didn't have an official name for them until the night we came across ladus at an ayurvedic restaurant, and he mistakenly proclaimed the name we now use for these tahini-based confections.*

---

1 cup raw, vegan granola, raw
   almonds or Gingersnaps (page 158)

1 (16-ounce) jar raw tahini

8 medjool dates,
   pitted and chopped

¼ cup maple syrup
   or brown rice syrup

¼ cup carob powder

½ cup currants or raisins

½ cup raw sunflower seeds

2 tablespoons raw cacao nibs

3 tablespoons minced
   crystallized ginger

1 tablespoon peeled
   and minced fresh ginger

1 teaspoon ground cinnamon

1 teaspoon ground cardamom

½ teaspoon ground cloves

⅛ teaspoon vanilla extract
   or cardamom extract

Pour the granola into a food processor. Process until finely ground. Transfer to a small bowl.

Put all the remaining ingredients in the food processor. Process until it is well mixed and forms a sticky mass, stopping occasionally to scrape down the work bowl. Alternatively, for a chunkier texture, mix all the remaining ingredients in a large bowl with a wooden spoon.

Roll the mixture into 1-inch balls with your hands. Roll each ball in the ground granola until well coated. Place on a serving plate. Keep refrigerated. Stored in a covered container in the refrigerator, Dadus will keep for 4 to 6 weeks.

Note: These cookies are high in protein and essential fatty acids, making them extremely healthful in the "good fat" kind of way.

Indian Chocolate Shake

balances vata and kapha
increases pitta slightly

Preparation Time: 10 minutes
Yield: 1 serving

Traditional Indian spices and raw chocolate are combined in this sensational, high-protein shake. Drinking this is one of my favorite ways to start the day.

1 frozen banana, cut into 3 or
    4 pieces (omit or use half
    for kapha)

1 tablespoon flaxseeds or chia seeds

3 medjool dates, pitted

1 tablespoon grated fresh ginger

½ teaspoon vanilla bean powder
    or ½ teaspoon vanilla extract

½ teaspoon chili powder

2 teaspoons ground cinnamon

1 teaspoon ground ginger

⅛ teaspoon ground cloves

1 tablespoon raw cacao powder,
    cocoa powder, or carob powder

¼ cup raw almonds or raw walnuts

8 to 10 ounces water

Put all the ingredients in a blender. Process until smooth, stopping occasionally to scrape down the blender jar.

Vegan Black Bean Brownies

balances vata and pitta
increases kapha

Preparation Time: 1 hour
Yield: 12 (2-inch square) brownies

Am I allowed to talk about food orgasms? If you are anything like me, this is what these brownies will give you. Do as the Dalai Lama says: "Approach love and cooking [and these brownies] with reckless abandon."

½ cup plus 1 teaspoon coconut oil

1 cup raw walnuts, chopped

¼ cup instant herbal
coffee substitute

1 teaspoon ground cinnamon
or mace (optional)

½ teaspoon salt

2 tablespoons egg replacer

½ cup water

1 cup brown rice syrup or maple syrup

2 cups cooked black beans,
or 1 (15-ounce) can black beans,
drained and rinsed

1 tablespoon vanilla extract

3½ ounces dark chocolate
(70 percent or more cacao)

Preheat the oven to 325 degrees F. Line an 11 x 9-inch glass baking pan with parchment paper. Oil the parchment paper with 1 teaspoon of the coconut oil.

Combine ½ cup of the walnuts, the coffee, optional cinnamon, and salt in a large bowl. Set aside. Whisk the egg replacer with the water in a small bowl until smooth. Add the brown rice syrup to the egg replacer mixture. Mix well. Set aside.

Put the black beans, the remaining ½ cup of walnuts, and the vanilla extract in a food processor.

Break the chocolate into pieces and put them in the top of a double boiler with the remaining ½ cup of the coconut oil. Stir until the chocolate is melted. Pour the chocolate mixture into the food processor with the black bean mixture. Process until smooth, stopping occasionally to scrape down the work bowl. Pour the black bean mixture into the walnut mixture. Mix well. Stir in the egg replacer mixture.

Pour the batter into the prepared pan. Bake for 40 minutes, or until the brownies are almost set. Because this recipe lacks eggs and flour, the batter may still seem a little soupy after baking. Let the brownies cool. Refrigerate them for 20 minutes before cutting them into squares. Stored in a covered container in the refrigerator, Vegan Black Bean Brownies will keep for 3 weeks.

Dadus, page 150

Sandy Lane Cherry Pie, page 163

Chocolate Fondue

Preparation Time: 10 minutes
Yield: About 1 cup

This is one of the first desserts I created as an ayurvedic chef, and I still consider it a go-to treat when I want something sweet. Use it as a dip for fresh fruit, such as bananas and strawberries, or cookies, such as Gingersnaps (page 158).

---

2 tablespoons raw almond butter, raw tahini, or raw pumpkin seed butter

4 tablespoons carob powder or cocoa powder

3 tablespoons Almond Milk (page 34), Rice Milk (page 34), or prepared almond, rice, or hempseed milk

¼ cup maple syrup or brown rice syrup

Mix all the ingredients in a medium bowl until creamy, or until it reaches the consistency of brownie batter. The mixture may be a little sticky. Or, put all the ingredients in a blender. Process until it reaches desired consistency, stopping occasionally to scrape down the blender jar. If the mixture is too thick, add another tablespoon of the Almond Milk or maple syrup.

Variations: Any nut or seed butter will taste delicious in this recipe. Try mixing two varieties, such as 1 tablespoon of tahini with 1 tablespoon of almond butter, or 1 tablespoon of coconut butter with 1 tablespoon of walnut butter. Use carob powder for pitta, as it's more cooling, calming, and alkaline than cacao powder.

Raw Cookie Dough

Preparation Time: 5 minutes
Yield: About 1 cup

Here's a cookie dough you can eat and feel great about. Just resist the temptation to eat it all in one sitting.

8 medjool dates, pitted

¼ cup raw almonds or raw walnuts

¼ cup dark chocolate chips
   or raw cacao nibs

Pinch salt

Put all the ingredients in a food processor. Process for about 15 seconds, or until the mixture is well combined, stopping once to scrape down the work bowl. Stored in a covered container in the refrigerator, Raw Cookie Dough will keep for 1 month.

Variations: Substitute ½ cup of Date Paste (page 146) for the 8 medjool dates. To calm pitta and kapha, substitute ¼ cup raw sunflower seeds for the raw almonds.

Sweet Orange-Date Rolls

Preparation Time: 25 minutes
Yield: 12 rolls; 6 servings

For a dessert that is simple, easy to transport, and everyone will love, make these yummy and fabulous rolls.

---

12 medjool dates

**½ cup raw almond butter
or walnut butter**

**2 tablespoons freshly squeezed
orange juice**

**1 tablespoon brown rice syrup
or raw agave nectar**

**1 teaspoon minced fresh ginger
(optional)**

1 teaspoon ground ginger

½ teaspoon ground cardamom

**¼ cup unsweetened shredded
coconut (optional)**

12 mint leaves, for garnish

Cut a lengthwise slit in each date with a sharp knife. Do not cut all the way through the date. Remove the pit and open each date to form a little bowl or hollow. Set aside.

In a medium bowl, mix the almond butter, orange juice, brown rice syrup, fresh ginger, ground ginger, and cardamom until smooth. Spoon 1 teaspoon of the almond mixture into each date.

Pour the optional coconut into a small bowl. Gently press the filling side of each date into the coconut. Arrange on a plate. Garnish each date with 1 mint leaf if desired. Stored in a covered container in the refrigerator, Sweet Orange-Date Rolls will keep for two weeks.

Amazingly Awesome Pumpkin Sweet Bread

decreases vata
balances pitta
increases kapha

Preparation Time: 1 hour, 15 minutes
Yield: 2 loaves, or about 16 muffins

Baking in my Aunt Julie's kitchen is like heaven on earth, both for her company and the gorgeous cañoncito surroundings. She inspired this recipe. Maybe that's why this bread always comes out so phenomenally moist, sweet, and yummy, like cake.

Wet ingredients

2 tablespoons egg replacer

½ cup plus ⅔ cup water

1¼ cups maple syrup

**1½ cups dehydrated cane juice
or date sugar**

**¼ cup molasses or dehydrated
cane juice**

1 cup coconut yogurt

1 teaspoon vanilla extract

**2 cups cooked fresh pumpkin
or 1 (16-ounce) can pumpkin**

Preheat the oven to 350 degrees F. Oil two 8½ x 4½-inch glass loaf pans or two muffin pans with coconut oil.

For the wet ingredients, whisk the egg replacer with ½ cup of the water in a large bowl until smooth. Add the maple syrup, dehydrated cane juice, molasses, yogurt, the remaining ⅔ cup of water, the vanilla extract, and pumpkin. Mix with a wooden spoon until all of the wet ingredients are well combined.

Dry ingredients

3 cups gluten-free baking mix

½ cup almond meal

**1½ teaspoons xanthan gum
or tapioca flour**

**1 tablespoon ground ginger (omit
for pitta)**

1 tablespoon ground cinnamon

2 teaspoons ground nutmeg

1 teaspoon ground cloves

**1 teaspoon licorice root powder
or ground anise (optional)**

2 teaspoons baking soda

1½ teaspoons salt

**1 cup chopped walnuts, slivered
almonds, or crushed pecans
(optional)**

For the dry ingredients, sift the baking mix, almond meal, xanthan gum, ginger, cinnamon, nutmeg, cloves, optional licorice root powder, baking soda, and salt into a large bowl. Add the wet ingredients to the dry ingredients. Stir in the optional walnuts.

Divide the batter equally between the prepared loaf pans or among the muffin cups. Bake for 1 hour, or until a toothpick inserted into the centers comes out clean. For muffins, bake for about 50 minutes, or until a toothpick inserted into the centers comes out clean.

Gingersnaps

Preparation Time: 30 minutes
Yield: About 2 dozen cookies

Gingersnaps make the world a better place. This gluten-free version is a key ingredient for many of the delectable pies and cookies you'll find in this book.

½ cup coconut oil, softened

1½ cups gluten-free baking mix

½ cup almond meal or coconut flour

1 teaspoon xanthan gum
  or tapioca flour

1 tablespoon ground ginger (use 1
  teaspoon for pitta)

1 teaspoon ground allspice

1 teaspoon baking soda

½ teaspoon salt

½ tablespoon egg replacer

2 tablespoons water

¼ cup molasses

½ cup maple syrup

2 tablespoons grated fresh ginger

1 cup minced crystallized ginger

1 tablespoon lemon zest

1 tablespoon orange zest

¼ cup coconut sugar
  or dehydrated cane juice

Preheat the oven to 350 degrees F. Line a large baking sheet with parchment paper, oiled waxed paper, or a silicone baking mat. To melt the coconut oil, put it in a medium glass bowl on the warm stovetop.

Sift the baking mix, almond meal, xanthan gum, ground ginger, allspice, baking soda, and salt into a large bowl.

Whisk the egg replacer with the water in a small bowl until smooth. Add it to the coconut oil, along with the molasses, maple syrup, and fresh ginger. Pour the molasses mixture into the almond mixture. Stir in the crystallized ginger, lemon zest, and orange zest. Pour the coconut sugar into a separate small bowl.

Roll tablespoonfuls of the dough into balls with your hands. Roll them in the coconut sugar. Place them about 1 inch apart on the prepared baking sheet. Flatten each ball slightly with the palm of your hand. Bake for 8 to 10 minutes, or until the tops start to crack. Let cool before serving.

Note: Fresh ginger is best for vata, while kapha will thrive on ground ginger. Excessive amounts of ginger may aggravate pitta, so cut the amount of ginger in half for the fiery people in your life. Alternatively, add 2 tablespoons of fennel seeds to help cool and calm pitta.

Gingersnap Pie Crust

balances vata, pitta, and kapha

Preparation Time: 25 minutes
Yield: 1 (9-inch) pie crust

This gluten-free crust tastes great with so many pie fillings. Try it with Thankful Pie (page 162), as a crust for Chai-Chocolate Mousse (page 147), or paired with Strawberry-Rhubarb Pie (page 161).

---

3 tablespoon coconut butter, softened

3 tablespoon coconut oil, softened

2 cups crumbs of Gingersnaps (opposite page) or prepared vegan gingersnap cookies

2 tablespoons unsweetened shredded coconut

1 tablespoon fennel seeds (optional)

Preheat the oven to 350 degrees F. Oil a 9-inch glass pie pan with coconut oil. Set aside.

To soften the coconut butter and coconut oil, put them in a glass bowl. Put the bowl in a saucepan of hot water.

Meanwhile, put the Gingersnaps in a food processor. Process until thoroughly ground. Transfer the Gingersnap crumbs to a medium bowl. Stir in the coconut and optional fennel. Stir the coconut butter mixture into the Gingersnap mixture until thoroughly combined.

Pour the Gingersnap mixture into the prepared pie pan. Press the mixture evenly into the bottom and up the sides of the pan. Bake for 10 minutes.

Valentine Pie

Preparation Time: 45 minutes
Yield: 1 (9-inch) pie; 6 servings

DeAnna and I made this on a February night while making valentines and celebrating her new love, who is now her husband. We still talk about how good this pie is. It must be all the love that went into its conception.

---

1 Gingersnap Pie Crust (page 159)

3 tablespoons dehydrated cane juice or date sugar

1 teaspoon ground cinnamon

1 teaspoon ground cardamom

1 large pear, cut into long, thin slices

12 ounces fresh or frozen blueberries

2 tablespoons coconut butter, softened

Prepare the Gingersnap Pie Crust, preferably in a heart-shaped pie pan. Preheat the oven to 375 degrees F.

Mix the dehydrated cane juice, cinnamon, and cardamom in a small bowl. Set aside.

Place 1 layer of the pear slices in the bottom of the pie crust, using half the pear slices. Place half the blueberries over the pears. Sprinkle 2 tablespoons of the cinnamon mixture over the blueberries. Repeat layers.

Bake for 30 minutes. Top each serving with 1 teaspoon of the softened coconut butter.

Strawberry-Rhubarb Pie

decreases vata
balances pitta
increases kapha

Preparation Time: 1 hour, plus overnight marinating time
Yield: 1 (9-inch) pie

Botanically a vegetable, yet considered a fruit in America (because we like it so much in pie), rhubarb is tart and best for vata or pitta when sweetened. This recipe is an adaptation of cookbook author Margaret S. Fox's brilliant "Rhubarb Glop." Choose rhubarb stalks that are thick, juicy, and sturdy.

---

12 stalks rhubarb (about 1 pound), cut into ½-inch pieces

2 (3-inch) cinnamon sticks (optional)

½ cup raw agave nectar or maple syrup

1 Gingersnap Pie Crust (page 159)

¼ cup dehydrated cane juice, jaggery or molasses

1 teaspoon lemon zest

2 tablespoons freshly squeezed lemon juice

2 tablespoons grated fresh ginger

1 teaspoon ground cardamom

2 cups fresh or frozen strawberries, sliced

Mix the rhubarb, cinnamon sticks, and agave nectar in a large bowl. Cover. Refrigerate overnight. Prepare the Gingersnap Pie Crust. Set aside.

Preheat the oven to 350 degrees F.

Combine the dehydrated cane juice with the rhubarb mixture. Place a colander over a large saucepan. Drain the rhubarb mixture in the colander. Transfer the rhubarb back into the bowl. Boil the rhubarb juice over medium-high heat for 5 minutes. Pour the juice over the rhubarb. Set aside for 15 minutes.

Stir the rhubarb mixture. Place the colander over a bowl. Drain the rhubarb mixture in the colander again. Pour ½ cup of the juice into the saucepan. (Use any remaining juice as a liquid sweetener for other recipes.) Transfer the rhubarb to the saucepan. Add the lemon zest, lemon juice, ginger, and cardamom. Cook the rhubarb mixture over medium-low heat, stirring occasionally, for 10 minutes, or just until the rhubarb is softened but not mushy. Let cool for 10 minutes.

Stir in the sliced strawberries. Pour the filling into the Gingersnap Pie Crust. Bake for 10 minutes.

Rhubarb Compote Variation: (decreases vata, increases pitta and kapha): The pie filling also makes a delicious topping for pancakes and waffles.

Thankful Pie

Preparation Time: 1 hour, 30 minutes
Yield: Filling for 2 (9-inch) pies

Revolutionize Thanksgiving with this nourishing, homemade pie of goodness. You can use almost any winter squash. They all work well and taste terrific.

---

2 Gingersnap Pie Crusts (page 159)

1½ tablespoons egg replacer

⅓ cup water

2 cups cooked and peeled butternut squash

1 cup coconut yogurt

½ cup maple syrup
   or brown rice syrup

2 tablespoons dehydrated cane juice
   or date sugar

2 tablespoons molasses, maple syrup,
   or Jerusalem artichoke syrup

1 tablespoon ground cinnamon

1 teaspoon ground ginger

1 teaspoon ground cardamom

½ teaspoon ground coriander

½ teaspoon ground nutmeg or mace

Prepare the Gingersnap Pie Crusts. Set aside.

Preheat the oven to 350 degrees F.

Whisk the egg replacer with the water in a small bowl until smooth. Pour it into a food processor or blender with the squash. Process just until combined. Add all the remaining ingredients. Process until smooth, stopping occasionally to scrape down the work bowl. Pour equally into the two Gingersnap Pie Crusts. Bake for 50 minutes, or until the fillings are firm.

Note: This pie is sensational with Almond Dream Cream (page 146) and a pinch of freshly ground pepper.

Sandy Lane Cherry Pie

decreases vata
increases pitta
balances kapha

Preparation Time: 30 minutes

Yield: 1 (9-inch) pie

SEE PHOTO FACING PAGE 153.

At our last "family" dinner, my friends unanimously voted this the best cherry pie ever.

Filling

1 pound ripe cherries, pitted, or frozen pitted cherries, thawed

¼ cup coconut sugar or dehydrated cane juice

¼ cup arrowroot starch

Juice of 1 lemon

1 tablespoon lecithin powder (optional)

Crust

2 tablespoons coconut oil

½ cup raw almonds or Brazil nuts

2 cups crushed Gingersnaps (page 158) or prepared gingersnap cookie crumbs

Pinch salt

Preheat the oven to 350 degrees F. To soften the coconut oil, put it on the warm stovetop. Oil a 9-inch glass pie pan with 1 teaspoon of the coconut oil.

To make the filling, bring the cherries, sugar, arrowroot, and lemon juice to a boil in a large saucepan over medium heat. Decrease the heat. Simmer, stirring constantly, for 5 minutes, or until the cherries release their juice and the sauce thickens. Remove from the heat. Stir in the optional lecithin. Set aside.

To make the crust, pour the almonds, gingersnaps, and salt into a food processor or blender. Process until ground to a coarse meal, stopping occasionally to scrape down the work bowl. Add the remaining coconut oil and process again briefly. Reserve ½ cup of the gingersnap mixture. Pour the remaining mixture into the prepared pie pan. Press the mixture evenly into the bottom and up the sides of the pan. Pour in the cherry filling. Sprinkle the reserved ½ cup of gingersnap mixture over the top. Bake for 10 minutes, or until the gingersnap topping is golden brown.

Note: Initially, I was daunted by the task of pitting so many cherries. But then I found such a simple way to do it that I actually look forward to it now. Here's how: Remove the stem of the cherry. Hold a chopstick in one hand and the cherry in your other hand. The little indentation where the stem meets the fruit is where you will pit the cherry. Jab the cherry's indentation with the tip of the chopstick, being careful not to poke yourself. If you aim it right, the cherry's pit will pop right out through the other end. A cherry pitter works, too; I'm just a rebel.

Glossary

Acid foods: Some foods can create an acidic pH level in body cells, fluid, and tissues. This makes the intake of health-giving oxygen and nutrients more difficult. Additionally, toxins cannot readily be removed. Most meats, nuts, grains, and sweeteners are acidic and should be eaten in moderation.

Agave nectar: Agave nectar is a liquid sweetener that comes from the agave plant. Use raw agave nectar whenever possible; other agave nectars sometimes contain additives and other sweeteners.

Agni: Agni is the ayurvedic term for digestive fire, or how well the digestive system is working. When agni is strong, food is digested properly, and you feel light and healthy. When agni is weak, toxins from undigested food may cause you to feel heavy or sluggish. Agni can be stimulated through the use of certain spices and fresh herbs.

Alkaline foods: Alkalizing foods can restore health to bodily tissues by bringing down the acidic pH level. Most fruits and vegetables are alkaline and should make up the bulk of your diet.

Astringency: In ayurveda, astringency represents the taste of air and earth. It is cold and tonifying. Tastes associated with astringency—such as pomegranate seeds, raspberries, and beans—balance pitta and kapha and unbalance vata.

Bitter: In ayurveda, bitter represents the taste of air and ether. It is cold and dry. Tastes associated with bitter—such as kale, cilantro, and aloe vera juice—balance pitta and kapha and unbalance vata.

Chlorophyll: Abundant in leafy green vegetables, sea vegetables, wheatgrass, and algae, chlorophyll is a regenerative, alkalizing, green pigment. It supports the body's immune system and helps the body detoxify and rebuild red blood cells.

Coconut: Young coconuts, also called Thai coconuts, are smooth, stout, and white, with a shaved, pointed top. They contain an electrolyte-rich "water" or "juice," and flesh or "meat" commonly used in raw food preparation. Mature coconuts are round, brown, and hairy, and their juice and meat are thicker. Coconuts are available in Asian markets and most natural food stores.

Dehydrated cane juice: A minimally processed cane sugar, dehydrated cane juice, unlike most refined and processed sugars, retains the naturally occurring molasses content, vitamins, and minerals found in sugar cane. These recipes were tested using Sucanat brand, which is available in natural food stores and in many major supermarkets.

Dinosaur kale: Also known as lacinato kale, dinosaur kale has deeply textured, dark green-blue leaves. The leaf is less rigid than some other varieties, making it useful in many salads and stir-fries.

Dosha: In ayurveda, the doshas are three biologically based, constitutional types known as vata, pitta, and kapha. They tend to go out of balance easily, which can result in physical symptoms or illness. Ayurveda is a science dedicated to keeping the doshas balanced through the proper application of food, nutrition, exercise, and lifestyle. Your specific balance of doshas is called your prakruti.

Egg replacer: Egg replacer is a powdered vegan egg substitute. Several brands are available. I recommend Ener-G Egg Replacer, made from potato starch.

Essential fatty acids: The body can easily use most of the fats it needs, but there are two it cannot synthesize—linoleic and alpha-linolenic—so the body must obtain them through food high in omega-3 and omega-6 fatty acids. Good sources include raw nuts, raw seeds, and cold-pressed oils.

GMO (genetically modified organism): GMO foods are grown from genetically engineered plants and seeds. (See page 27.)

Grounding: When a food or a dish is "grounding," it means it is calming and comforting for the body. To be "grounded" is to be down to earth and to feel in touch with your body and your emotions.

Gunas: Gunas are attributes or qualities found in the five elements of nature—ether, air, fire, water, and earth—as they are expressed through the doshas. (See page 1.)

Kapha: One of the three doshas, with vata and pitta, kapha represents the union of water and earth.

Lecithin powder: Lecithin is an emulsifier that helps thicken and bind ingredients such as oil and water. Lecithin powder is finer in texture and tastier than granules. Look for vegan lecithin since some is derived from eggs. I recommend Non-GMO Lecithin Powder by Healthforce Nutritionals (see page 169).

Low-glycemic foods: A low-glycemic food does not spike a sharp release of glucose into the blood. Examples of low-glycemic foods include raw nuts and seeds, barley, brown rice, and stevia.

Maca root powder: Maca is a hardy, cruciferous root vegetable with a sweet and pungent taste. It is known to support immune health and balance hormones. It is interchangeable with maca flour.

Mineralizing: Mineralizing refers to foods that are hydrating and rich in minerals necessary to create electrolyte balance in the body.

Miso: Miso is fermented soybean paste, used as a base or seasoning in soups, sauces, and dressings. Lighter-colored miso tastes sweeter and more mellow than stronger, darker miso.

Neem: A bitter, cooling ayurvedic herb grown in India, neem is best known for its antifungal and anti-inflammatory properties.

Nut milk bag: Also called a sprouting bag, a nut milk bag is a fine cloth strainer that hangs over the edge of a bowl or pitcher to drain nut and grain milks. Alternatively, a bag of double-folded cheesecloth can be used.

Nutritional yeast flakes: Nutritional yeast flakes are a form of deactivated yeast that lends a cheese-like flavor to foods. They are often fortified with B vitamins.

Ojas: A Sanskrit term literally translated as "vigor," ojas represents the strength of the body's vital fluids, such as blood and reproductive fluids. The quality of ojas is representative of your overall health, immunity, wellness, and vitality.

Pitta: One of the three doshas, with vata and kapha, pitta represents the elements of fire and water.

Prakruti: In ayurveda, prakruti is your innate, elemental, and predominant constitution, or dosha. For most of us, the unique combination of elements present at birth are genetically and karmically determined and do not change throughout your life.

Probiotic: Rich in beneficial bacteria for the colon, probiotics may be found in foods such as coconut kefir, coconut yogurt, raw sauerkraut, and prepared probiotic beverages and supplements.

Pungent: Pungency represents the taste of air and fire. It is hot and stimulating. Tastes associated with pungency, such as garlic, ginger, and basil, balance kapha but unbalance pitta and vata.

Rajas: One of the three gunas (with sattva and tamas), rajas is the active, kinetic quality of life, the force of movement. There are rajasic, or active, qualities inherent in each of the three doshas.

Rasa: Rasa is the initial experience of taste, when something is first placed on the tongue. The six rasas are sweet, salty, sour, bitter, pungent, and astringent.

Rejuvelac: A restorative beverage made from fermented grain, rejuvelac is considered a digestive aid and a source of probiotics.

Salty: Salt represents the taste of fire and water. It is warm and moist. Tastes associated with salt, such as sea vegetables, celery, and tamari, balance vata and unbalance pitta and kapha.

Sattva: One of the three gunas (with rajas and tamas), sattva is the pure, balanced quality of existence. Sattvic foods are balancing for all doshas.

Sour: In ayurveda, sour represents the taste of fire and earth—hot, light, and wet. Tastes associated with sour, such as lemon, tomato, and vinegar, balance vata but unbalance pitta and kapha and should be eaten in moderation.

Superfoods: Superfoods are known for their remarkable health benefits and high levels of bio-available micronutrients.

Sweet: Sweet represents the taste of water and earth. It is rich and heavy. Tastes associated with sweet, such as rice, squash, and sweet potatoes, balance vata and pitta but can unbalance kapha.

Tamas: One of the three gunas (with rajas and sattva), tamas represents the dull, inert, destructive quality of nature.

Tonic: Tonics are usually sweet, heavy, and nourishing foods, drinks, herbs, and teas. Their primary function is to increase vital bodily fluids, such as blood, lymph, and reproductive fluids. They strengthen, invigorate, and restore health to organs, tissues, and mucous membranes, and restore health and balance to our organs.

Vata: One of the three doshas (with pitta and kapha), vata represents the elements of air and ether.

Vipak: Vipak is the long-term impact a food or taste has on the body after chewing, absorption, and assimilation.

Virya: Virya refers to the heating or cooling effect a food, herb, or spice has on the body after it's ingested.

Resources

Do all you can
With what you have
In the time you have
In the place you are.
— Nkosi Johnson

Ingredients

Banyan Botanicals
banyanbotanicals.com
Ayurvedic herbs, spices, and herbal
remedies

Bob's Red Mill
bobsredmill.com
Gluten-free, all-purpose baking mix,
amaranth flour, almond meal, arrowroot,
brown rice flour, buckwheat groats,
coconut flour, garbanzo bean flour, oat
groats, gluten-free rolled oats, tapioca
flour, and more

Coconut Secret
coconutsecret.com
Coconut nectar, vinegar, aminos, sugar,
and flour

Divine Organics/Transition Nutrition
divineorganics.com
transitionnutrition.com
Raw cacao nibs, goji berries, certified
organic extra-virgin coconut oil, Irish moss,
mulberries, Himalayan crystal salt, purple
olives, pure raw agave nectar

Ener-G Foods, Inc.
ener-g.com
Gluten-free Ener-G Egg Replacer

Follow Your Heart
Followyourheart.com
Vegenaise (prepared vegan mayonnaise),
vegan Cheddar cheese, Monterey jack
cheese, and sour cream

Healthforce Nutritionals

healthforce.com

Vegan, raw, superfoods, including blue-green algae, sprouted chia and flaxseeds, non-GMO lecithin powder, Spirulina Manna, Vitamineral Green, maca powder, and vegan probiotics.

Mountain Rose Herbs

mountainroseherbs.com

Bulk organic herbs, cinnamon chips, organic culinary oils, lavender essential oil, and salt

Premier Organics

premierorganics.org

Artisana raw nut and seed butters, including raw almond butter, coconut butter, raw tahini, and raw extra-virgin coconut oil starter kits

Rejuvenative Foods

rejuvenation.com

Raw organic nut and seed butters, kimchee, and raw sauerkraut

Rising Tide Sea Vegetables

loveseaweed.com

All types of raw, wild seaweed, and Sea Crunchies (toasted sea palm)

South River Miso Company

southrivermiso.com

Handmade, artisan miso

The Raw Diet Health Shop

therawdiet.com

Nut milk bags, sauerkraut crocks, blenders, juicers, dehydrators, rice cookers, water filters, grain mills, spiral slicers (for making raw vegetable pasta), and dairy-free kefir starter

Educational Resources

dhyana Center of Health Sciences

dhyanacenter.com

DeAnna Batdorff, founder

Offers ayurvedic education, ayurvedic certification programs, pancha karma, ayurvedic tools for wellness, and ayurvedic treatments.

Aushadi Health Foundation

aushadihealth.com

An educational nonprofit offering low-cost ayurveda-by-donation clinics; community classes; and the Sonoma County Community Kitchen and Flourish Café, educating and feeding people in need. All donations go toward community education through the heart of ayurveda.

Donations are accepted at the website.

Kripalu School of Ayurveda

kripalu.org

Open to anyone interested in ayurvedic medicine, Kripalu is located in the Berkshires of Western Massachusetts. It offers ayurvedic lifestyle consultant certifications, ayurvedic yoga specialist certifications, and foundations of ayurveda.

Mount Madonna Institute College of Ayurveda

mountmadonnainstitute.org/ayurveda

Located in the beautiful Santa Cruz Mountains and modeled after the Bachelor of Ayurvedic Medicine and Surgery curriculums in India. Ayurveda courses are taught by experts in each subject so that students gain a variety of perspectives.

Talya's Kitchen

talyaskitchen.com

Hands-on cooking classes, ayurvedic cleansing programs, natural food store tours, catering, personal chef services, ayurvedic consultations, ayurvedic massage, pancha karma, and yoga classes

The Ayurvedic Institute

ayurveda.com

Doctor Vasant Lad, founder

A nonprofit organization established in 1984 to teach the traditional ayurvedic medicine of India and to provide these ancient therapies in the US. The institute provides authentic education that encourages the integration of ayurveda into daily living and offers ayurvedic healing through herbs, nutrition, pancha karma cleansing, acupressure massage, yoga, Sanskrit, and jyotish (vedic astrology).

Index

NOTE: Recipe names appear in *italics*.

About the Author

Talya Lutzker is a certified ayurvedic practitioner, certified massage practitioner, yoga teacher, professional chef, and the founder of Talya's Kitchen, an organic, nutrition-focused catering business.

Specializing in ayurveda since 2003, Talya offers personalized nutrition consultations, personal chef services, catering, natural food store tours, ayurvedic massage, pancha karma, and yoga classes. Her popular cooking classes inspire people to deepen their self-care and find joy in the kitchen. Catch Talya's Kitchen cooking segments on her website and YouTube.com.

Talya's passion for holistic medicine and innovative, healthful cooking sparkles in her lively and entertaining teaching style and shines through everything she does. She has studied with DeAnna Batdorff, founder of the dhyana Center of Health Sciences, since 2001 and has a bachelor's degree in environmental studies from the University of California in Santa Barbara.

To learn more about Talya and Talya's Kitchen, please visit talyaskitchen.com or Talya's Kitchen on Facebook.

BookPublishing Co.

books that educate, inspire, and empower

Visit BookPubCo.com to find your favorite books on
plant-based cooking and nutrition, raw foods, and healthy living.

Anti-Inflammatory
Foods and Recipes
Beverly Lynn Bennett
978-1-57067-341-2
$17.95

Low-FODMAP and Vegan
Jo Stepaniak, MSEd
978-1-57067-337-5
$17.95

Beauty by Nature
Brigitte Mars
978-1-57067-193-7
$19.95

Bravo!
Chef Ramses Bravo,
with Alan Goldhamer
978-1-57067-269-9
$19.95

Herbal Antivirals
Sorrel Davis
978-1-57067-344-3
$12.95

Vegan Fitness For Mortals
Ellen Jaffe Jones
978-1-57067-340-5
$14.95

Purchase these titles from your favorite book source or buy them directly from:
Book Publishing Company • P.O. Box 99 • Summertown, TN 38483 • 1-888-260-8458

Free shipping and handling on all book orders.